GW01238471

A Guide to Creative Writing

Other Titles From This Author

Dicing With Danger
Jenna's Dad
Guardian Angel
I've Got a Pen and I'm Not Afraid to Use it (Second Edition)
Writing Naked
Ghosting!
Livin' and Lovin' in Texas
Dream State

A Guide to Creative Writing

SJ Banham

WHITE OWL

AN IMPRINT OF PEN & SWORD BOOKS LTD.
YORKSHIRE – PHILADELPHIA

First published in Great Britain in 2024 by
White Owl
An imprint of
Pen & Sword Books Ltd.
Yorkshire - Philadelphia

Copyright © SJ Banham, 2024

ISBN 978 1 39903 514 9

The right of SJ Banham to be identified as author of this work has been asserted by her in accordance with the Copyright, Designs and Patents Act 1988.

A CIP catalogue record for this book is available from the British Library.

All rights reserved. No part of this book may be reproduced or transmitted in any form or by any means, electronic or mechanical including photocopying, recording or by any information storage and retrieval system, without permission from the Publisher in writing.

Typeset in INDIA by IMPEC eSolutions
Printed and bound in the UK on paper from a sustainable source by
CPI Group (UK) Ltd., Croydon. CR0 4YY.

Pen & Sword Books Ltd. incorporates the imprints of Pen & Sword Books:
After the Battle, Archaeology, Atlas, Aviation, Battleground, Discovery,
Family History, History, Maritime, Military, Politics, Select, Transport, True Crime,
Fiction, Frontline Books, Leo Cooper, Praetorian Press, Seaforth Publishing,
Wharncliffe and White Owl.

For a complete list of Pen & Sword titles please contact

PEN & SWORD BOOKS LIMITED
George House, Beevor Street, Off Pontefract Road, Hoyle Mill, Barnsley,
South Yorkshire, England, S71 1HN.
E-mail: enquiries@pen-and-sword.co.uk
Website: www.pen-and-sword.co.uk

or

PEN AND SWORD BOOKS
1950 Lawrence Rd, Havertown, PA 19083, USA
E-mail: uspen-and-sword@casematepublishers.com
Website: www.penandswordbooks.com

Contents

Contents

Introduction and Acknowledgements

Stories can be incredible. They can be entertaining, and they can be life changing. Fiction can take you to other worlds or help keep your feet firmly planted on Earth. Poetry helps your soul to soar, and non-fiction can empower you towards personal development or keep you informed within your career's industry. At its bare bones, creative writing can change the world. And that is not even too dramatic a description either.

I distinctly remember the moment I learned to read inside my head rather than out loud. My sister was a big reader and I wanted to be just like her – what younger sibling doesn't? The fact that I could finally do this fascinated me. The transference of speaking the words aloud to just hearing them inside my head blew my mind. After a few attempts, I could do it without realising.

I also distinctly recall the moment in my school classroom that I learned how to write words and separate each one using my finger to space them across the page. I had terrible trouble with that at first, which I suspect is why my teacher told me to use my finger. Learning how each word was constructed with (what seemed like) so many letters in each meant the words blurred into one, line upon line. The page I was given to practise on was physically huge, too. Its sheen stopped the pencil working efficiently, and the pencil itself was scratchy, leaving sharp indentations on the page and letters with missing parts. Looking back, the whole process seemed unnecessarily unhelpful for very young minds to learn how to write. In retrospect, it feels like we were given more challenges than help, but none of this seems to have put me off my love of words and storytelling. I may have had difficulty in creating individual words back then, but my passion for creating material from them has increased.

Afterwards, my interest in letters and words began. I enjoyed the way they were shaped in different fonts and colours for different books, which seemed to give different feelings and meanings, even though I didn't fully understand authors' or publishers' intentions back then. I didn't even know what an author or publisher was. Later, I found I would return to the same few books all the time. I still don't know if that was because they were exciting stories, or if it was down to the familiarity of the cover, words, and pictures. They were enough to provide a safe, comforting feeling giving me, a young reader, a good night's sleep.

The idea that books could be exciting or thrilling came to me in my teenage years. My mother's love of romantic stories meant she would take a few novels away on family holidays to log cabins or caravans to give her something to do when we were out exploring the surroundings. Those few hours alone would give her the me-time and escapism she needed. But it was my curious mind that made me pick up one or two and read snippets from them.

As a teenager, I didn't have a big attention span (I still don't), so reading a chapter here or a snippet there and glossing through to the end to see how the characters ended up was my way of learning what kept my mother's interest. I generally took a notebook and pen away on holiday with me, so once or twice I tried to start my own novel. I quite liked the idea of storytelling, making up fancy names of characters and giving each of them a job to carry out. I would get confused as to how much detail ought to go into the story, or how little. Should I write that they sat down on a chair, or turned a door handle to get into the room like we do in real life? Should I write what colour the car was, or if they changed gear from second to third as they drove to the millionaire's mansion? Or how loud the engine was, or what kind of fuel it took to make the thing go in the first place? How much was too much detail and how much was not enough? After an hour so of getting lost in the detritus of unnecessary details and achieving little, and with no real understanding or plan of what I was meant to do, nor having the stamina to get it done, I would get bored super-quickly. Downing tools, I would go do something else instead and there ended my wander into creative writing for the day.

Much later I saw what other people got from giving a story a chance. I learned that words were more than just the things we had no choice but to read at school, they were tiny pieces of artwork that joined together like jigsaw pieces. I began taking an interest, jotting down poems by way of letting out weird thoughts (also known as puberty) and, an old school friend recently reminded me, I wrote a few would-be scripts that were episodes of TV shows I liked. When I left school, I tried my hand at a few short stories and then, in my twenties, I wrote a full-length novel that would now be referred to today as fan fiction. Back then the genre of fan fiction wasn't yet known as it is today. I enjoyed writing about existing characters while creating a few more and, better yet, spending as much time with them as I could as though it was real life. That book took me eighteen months to write and takes forty-five minutes to read. I still have it somewhere. It serves as a physical reminder of my literary apprenticeship.

Reaching almost four decades into my writing career, I realise now that I began with a decade of getting my writing completely wrong. That is, nothing I wrote conveyed what I wanted it to. It sounded weak or too aggressive, too comical when I needed to be serious, too serious when a bit of light-heartedness was needed. Even when I wrote non-fiction, I seemed to quickly lose the point I was making, or I could not easily find any theme within the piece. That was both my inexperience and poor attention span kicking in. The countless feelings I experienced while writing fiction, that I tried to show through my characters, were electric, yet on the page their faces barely exhibited any emotion. They were wooden in the reading, like insipid drawings, flat and lifeless. Why wouldn't they jump from the page and become real people like they did in the books my mother read? It was demoralising. So how did authors do it? What was their secret?

I need not have worried because I wasn't really getting anything wrong at all. I was simply learning. I can say that now because retrospective self-reflection is helpful. At the time, I had no idea I could even be a writer let alone continue doing it as a career. Nobody is born knowing it all. Everything we try takes time to learn, from the basics upwards, and it was this I needed to appreciate and understand. It just took intention, determination, and patience. You can argue it also takes discipline and tenacity too, but for now focusing upon one or two needs is key.

A career in writing wasn't even a choice open to me back when I left school because I had heard from my careers officer that to be a writer you must have lots of qualifications and money. I had neither. I often wonder how many young minds are thrown off their intended path because of one person's ill-conceived thoughts influencing them.

It wasn't until my thirties that I realised no matter what my day job was, my career was always going to be writing. It wasn't that writing came easily to me, it was more about how natural it felt to do it. It was when I expressed myself through fiction, non-fiction, occasional poetry, and comic verse that I realised not only did it feel as natural as breathing to me, but I could also turn what I now knew into a business enveloping each skill that was now second nature to me. I could offer a service, helping others almost fast track their development rather than go through the rough stuff I had. Sure, they also needed to learn aspects the hard way as they saw it, but if I could help empower them or instil a little confidence at first, they would learn what they wanted to a lot quicker than I had. Where most of my early learning was hindered by lack of self-confidence, theirs would be enveloped and protected through empowerment. If I could help new writers feel that sooner rather than later, I had done a good job.

Becoming a professional writer was one of the most significant decisions of my life because it meant I wasn't just doing it for enjoyment or curiosity's sake anymore, it now had a financial value attached. At that point, I learned the difference between writing for love and writing for money. For some people, it affects the outcome. Adjusting this thought process meant I could do both. It was all about learning, being patient, and a lot of self-nurturing, just like I believe we ought to do when learning about creative writing in the first place.

We often put pressure on ourselves to get the thing we are doing right first time. If we don't achieve that perfection straight away, in our current culture of instancy, we may cast it aside, never again bothering with it. But the creativity within writing means there's not really any way of getting it wrong. It's *creative* writing for a reason. If that pressure is removed, and your expectations are managed, you can write purely for the enjoyment, allowing improvement later should that become necessary or if the goal posts change. In that case, we may even produce a result even better than that originally planned.

From that little girl learning to read in the early 1970s to a middle-aged woman being awarded a degree in English Literature and Creative Writing in 2022, it is clear to me that some of us are late developers, and a lot of that is down to confidence. Rather a lack of confidence. Whatever age you are and whatever you want to write, I am here to tell you that you can do it. With a little help, some guidance, and plenty of reassurance, you can absolutely write that story, that memoir, that self-help book, or that poem.

For helping me create this book, my thanks go to my husband Robert, and our daughter Chloe, both for their continued support with all my literary projects. To my parents Jo and Stan Stuart for always cheering me on in life, and in my career. To my sister, Suzy Buttress, whose chats about nature and birds constantly helps to lifts my spirits, and who helped me learn how to read inside my head. To Jimmie Bise for his invaluable help with this book, and to fellow authors: Bryan Lightbody, Henry Hyde, Sarah Dodd, members of Alliance of Independent Authors, Society of Authors, and Arcane Quill for many a pick-me-up and literary conversation. To those at White Owl and Pen and Sword, thank you.

Preface

With so many books on the topic of creative writing out there in the world, it does make you wonder what else can be covered. But while many look mostly at the mechanics of writing, very few include nurturing the new writer, reassuring the hesitant writer, providing stimulus to the curious writer, or even highlighting some of the pitfalls writers face while creating. I believe that is where this book sits. Sometimes, especially in this age of instant and often harsh rhetoric, a little gentle guidance from someone who has been there themselves can be welcome when deconstructing topics to their bones before rebuilding them. Therefore, this guide is intended to speak to those just starting to scratch the surface of creative writing as well as those who have already spent years writing stories and non-fiction alike.

When we are drawn to an activity, we want to dedicate all our free time into it so we can indulge for hours, days, even weeks at a time. But if you are not sure where to start or, indeed, how to start, learning can become tricky, and so can the amount of time we need to allow in our schedule. Some of us simply give up, focusing our attention elsewhere and deeming the activity too hard for the time available. At this point we are not even sure if it will become a much-loved hobby, or simply something we tried once; reminiscing with teary eyes because we wanted to give it another go but, recalling how tough it was, what was the point? But creative hobbies need not be hard to learn because, by their very nature, they allow understanding simply by doing, by giving it a go. Creativity involves imagination and a willingness to create. So, if you want to do something creative and exercise your imagination, you have found the right book for you.

As children, we learn by having a go, yet as adults there is often a sense of needing to get it right first time. Even when time is scarce, we still expect this accuracy. It makes sense, of course. If we have just one hour of free time, we may not want to spend it learning about something when we could actually be doing it. Children, therefore, probably enjoy activities more because they are not presented with the restrictions of perfection or expectation, while, as adults we may feel as if we have failed before we have begun. I believe we can learn a lot from the enquiring nature of a child's mind. Wouldn't it be wonderful to remind ourselves what it feels like to simply enjoy an activity by having a go? Of course, there will always be an opportunity to improve the project later in whichever way you deem fit and for whatever outcome you had hoped.

The word nurture is often afforded to children and their development but applying it to your own, within a creative writing project, fits perfectly because it means you will view the project in a different way. I have discovered over time that removing pressure in whichever form it takes and replacing it with nurture, that is encouraging the development of the project, is more beneficial for a good result. It took me a lot of years to realise this, and even more to put it in place. But you don't have to wait that long.

Nurturing your creative development instantly puts a different frame around it, enveloping the project in a safer, more enjoyable mindset. Doing this also gives you a 'get out of jail free' card by way of allowing yourself to make errors. And while errors are our way of learning and developing, not everyone realises this. Without errors, we cannot improve. To be reprimanded for an error can create an environment of anxiety in some, and rebellion or a refusal to learn in others. But wouldn't it be wonderful to learn without the worry of the repercussions of errors, and even to invite them so we can view the project both ways? Surely then, this method can lead to confidence and empowerment that, in turn, will take you into a completely different mindset where many more things can be achieved, all because of the initial nurturing.

You don't need to be a particularly creative person to write, nor do you need to have a logical or artistic mind. You don't need to be an introvert or extrovert, or, indeed, any specific kind of person at all. All you really need is intention. Once you have made the decision to write, anything else you need will be along soon enough because the intent is there.

So, the decision is made and you want to write. What now? And that's where this book comes in. Within these pages, you'll discover tools to help you write that may never have crossed your mind before, including word prompts, exercises that help release the bars on your imagination, and practical tips to aid your daily mindset and creative point of view, all wrapped up in an upbeat, easy-to-read conversational tone. However, while the primary focus of this guide is to empower the new writer, there are sections that will revitalise experienced ones. If you have ever put down your pen through lack of confidence, not expecting to ever take hold of it again, know that you have found the right book to guide you back into expressing your creativity and imagination once more.

Creative writing is a versatile activity that aids you in all kinds of projects from keeping a diary or journal, staying in touch with loved ones, right up to creating a family heirloom, writing a novel or a piece of non-fiction, like recording a loved one's life story. And it doesn't stop there either. There are so many ways to use creative writing to achieve that special something, or to begin a new hobby.

Using my experience of guiding hesitant writers to transfer ideas they have been harbouring for years out of their heads and onto the page, I will walk you through some obvious steps of starting a creative writing project, a few not-so-obvious ones, and highlight prompts, tips, and tools that can motivate you towards getting it written.

Creating self-confidence and empowerment with and through creative writing is the essence of this guide. Engaging with our language is one of the most exciting and empowering activities we can do, because it doesn't just stop when you have completed your project, those skills will remain with you forever.

Whatever your intended writing project, *A Guide to Creative Writing* will assist you in achieving it. All you need to do is turn the page.

Chapter 1

The Excitement of Creative Writing

Have you ever walked through a book shop or library and just stared at the books as they line the shelf? Do you get caught up in the colours and shapes they create on that shelf, or are you more interested in the content beneath those covers? Or a particular author? Or perhaps the idea that somehow the author had you in mind when they wrote the book because all their other works have spoken directly to you? Do you ever linger at one specific part of the book shop or library because it holds the category you enjoy reading the most? Or do you browse for hours, teasing your imagination as to which book you will choose this time? Are you less drawn to a specific genre and more focused on reading everything that jumps out at you no matter what it is, purely for the love of absorbing its content?

For some, reading fiction is the golden ticket. Entering different worlds, different eras, prehistoric and futuristic alike, meeting characters who you would love to have as a best friend, or even imagining you are the protagonist of the story might be nothing short of a delight. Going on international adventures, falling in love, solving mysteries, discovering secrets, becoming a magician, a spy, an assassin, a king or queen, an animal, or an alien, may be your daily literary diet of choice, consuming the words like each one was your last meal. For others it is non-fiction where they find their true joy, where their reading hours are reserved for education, information, or entertainment. With an array of biographies, autobiographies, self-help books, textbooks, local, regional, or international history books, celebrity travel memoirs, environmental tomes, hobby and leisure books, business books or a multitude of other non-fiction reading materials lining the shelves, there is always something to feed your curiosity and thirst for knowledge.

When we choose a book from the shelves of a book shop or library, we usually pick it up because something about the look, size, or colour of it attracts us. The adage about judging a book by its cover is completely and utterly true whether we want to admit it or not. Colours, shapes, sizes, fonts, they all draw our attention. After the cover pulls us in, we may sneak a peek at the blurb to find out what the book is about. The price will then factor into our decision whether to buy it if we are in a bookshop. Finally, and this isn't something everyone does but certainly something I do, there is a quick gloss over of the first paragraph and – shock, horror – the final paragraph of a novel. Spoilers usually divide a room. All these (although probably minus the last one) will help you decide if you want this book. That, right there, is excitement. The excitement of anticipation. The excitement and choosing of a book can fill our minds. You may wonder if the story will live up to its brilliant blurb? Will the characters be how you hope they will? For those with enquiring, critical-thinking minds, you may be curious to know if the plot credits you with the ability to fill in some gaps, or will it be served on a platter then spoon fed to you? We'll touch on this thought later.

If reading a book someone else has written conjures that kind of excitement, imagine if you were the writer of your own book. Have you ever felt that you would like to write your own book? The mere fact that you have picked up this book suggests the answer is 'Yes'. Have you ever considered that if you took the plunge of writing your own what process you'd take, or what kind of story you might enjoy writing? It might be the kind you enjoy reading. Maybe the idea of writing non-fiction appeals? A business book perhaps? Self-help even, or a collection of your family's memories shaped into a legacy for future generations to read and treasure as an heirloom? Maybe those ideas motivate you enough to give it some serious thought?

So, what if you could create that excitement yourself? Rather than read someone else's book, what if you wrote your own? Often people confess they have wanted to write a book since they were a child. Some say they want to be a writer when they grow up, and it is a well-known thought that there is a book inside everyone. I tend to agree. I wonder, then, what has stopped you turning those thoughts into action? Did something run through your mind telling you that you couldn't? Or shouldn't? What was it that made you shelf your proactivity?

There are a myriad of excuses we give ourselves about why we won't do something. Some of these reasons could be the fear of the unknown, lack of time, lack of imagination, confusion about where to begin, decisions on how and where to research, beliefs that you will need expensive or specialist equipment, wondering if the book has to be published or if a handwritten one-off is a better idea for the project you want to do? Are you concerned it might read as boring? Or stupid? Are you concerned you don't have the energy? That you are not confident enough? Smart enough? All these queries, and more, and potential solutions are touched upon within this book.

Suffice to say that when a new writer begins a project, while there is much to consider, we do not have to consider it all at that moment we begin. That would feel too overwhelming. While some creative people are fuelled by logic, analytical and critical thinking, and using spreadsheets and fixed, rigid structures of processes and plans to write their books, others are motivated through and by their emotions, using handwritten notes within physical spiral-bound notebooks and working without a plan anywhere close by. And neither is right, yet both are right. Each completes their goal because each does it in a way that suits them, and their individual process.

There is a school of thought that reminds us that no matter what our experience, ability, or intention no one size fits all because, just like people, books and other original creative writing projects are all unique.

Creativity allows us to be as wild or as subtle as we need to be to get that idea out of our heads and hearts and into the world. And always remember, even if your creative writing project is not intended for the eyes of others, it matters not because it remains as unique as its creator. You.

Finding Your People

A few decades ago, before I really understood creative writing in the way I do now, but after I had written quite a few short stories, some poetry, and a couple of never-to-be-shared novels, I heard about a book festival that was to be held in a nearby library. I had no idea what to expect or what the format would be, but the idea of a festival celebrating books, authors, and stories was such an exciting prospect, yet I was quite apprehensive at the same time.

I believed book festivals were for very clever people and someone like me really ought not waste my time going. What would I expect to get out of it? I had no idea.

Even so, curiosity led me to the library the week beforehand to ask about it. One of the assistants asked me if I was a reader or was it the writing aspect I was drawn to. I told them I read a little and I wrote quite a bit. They asked in which genre I wrote, but that flummoxed me. I was not sure of the word 'genre'. I was stuck. I fumbled my answer, and the hesitation allowed them to jump in and to ask what I liked to read. I said I was drawn to romance novels. Unfortunately, they did not respond in a way that I believe to be helpful or encouraging, stating that the festival would be filled with those who wrote more highbrow books than that. They went on to tell me I might not get much out of the festival, effectively trying to talk me out of it (not a great marketing move on their part!). My curiosity got the better of me and, determined and persistent, I noted the date anyway and went along. Thankfully, I did.

On that day I realised that every workshop I attended excited me and everyone I met who wrote spoke my language. Having someone else to talk to about the highs and lows of creative writing was a blessing. I had no idea other people could appreciate the kind of apprehension or exhilaration I had felt when writing. Those I spoke to seemed to understand how some stories don't work as well as you had hoped, how what is on the page is not necessarily how it felt in your imagination, how excited you feel when a character blossoms before your eyes on the page, or how plots can sometimes take a few rewrites before they begin to sing – or even make logical sense. I heard people say they had written themselves into a corner they had no idea how to get out of, using their dreams as plots, or that through being in 'the zone' they had totally forgotten they were writing the story, feeling in fact as if they were living it instead.

These were my people.

I recall that in one workshop, a man lifted his hand to ask a question. 'What does genre mean?' he asked. I stared at him knowing I had similar questions and remembering that was how I stumbled in front of the library assistant. I believed I ought to know what that meant and many other things too. I believed that, perhaps, it had all been covered at school and I was fast asleep in the corner? I found myself afraid to ask questions in case I looked silly. It was this kind of thing that had kept me back for so long. But this man had been braver, enough in fact, to ask his question in front of a room filled with eager ears. When he asked that question, several other audience members nodded along with him. It appeared there were a lot of us in the room who wrote stories upon stories but didn't know aspects of creative writing others consider the basics. When the speaker explained genre simply meant 'category or type', there was an audible sound of understanding in the audience. It was that simple. It was just an industry word. At that point, I realised there were probably many more industry words I ought to learn just so it made things easier for me to grasp in future.

I remember phoning my husband later that day telling him how exciting the event had been and how everyone spoke my language. Just those few words seemed to allow everything I had been practising naturally all those years beforehand to simply click into place. Often it just takes one person to explain something in a way that is respectful, encouraging, and that hits the target instantly.

As my mother always told me, 'Nobody is born knowing everything. We all have to learn it from the ground upwards.' I realise now that some of us might miss the thing the first time around but pick it up later. Sometimes much later. Not knowing it straight away can lead to lack of confidence later, but remaining open-minded to learning throughout life can aid us. And, of course, if someone else asks the question, we might benefit from hearing the answer too.

After this event, I began looking for local writing groups. My hope was to join one and learn something about how other writers put their stories together, perhaps even make friends with like-minded individuals. Back then there seemed little in the way of local writers willing to highlight themselves. At this point, the internet as it is today did not exist, nor did social media. In fact, some years later, chat rooms became popular, which gives you an idea of the era. Had the internet existed like it does now, and social media too, I would have easily jumped onto the computer and cast my net wide to see who I could catch with similar interests. Instead, I relied on my local library, nearby bookshops, and word of mouth in the area. The library staff said they did not currently have a writing group, so why didn't I start one? I was not sure about that. It seemed like it might take a lot of work I did not know about, and highlighted me within the community that, as an occasional introvert, worried me. Having a chat with the teachers at my daughter's school helped a little with the idea and, occasionally, I was asked to come in to help the children with their reading and learn their spellings, which I really enjoyed.

I gave it some more thought. This went on for weeks. It was then that I decided – in my naively curious way – to put an advert in the village magazine calling for others who enjoyed creative writing to join me in the beer garden at a local pub one summer evening. It was a long shot to expect anyone to show up, but five others joined me, all diverse in age, ranging from school-aged teens right through to an octogenarian. From those people from different walks of life, creative writing became somewhat of a leveller. It did not matter what we knew or what we did not know, it was more about how much we had in common within each other and how many social barriers were being broken. It gave us all a real sense of community, with creative writing at the centre.

For a year we remained together and became ambitious with our writing goals. As a group we created a collection of short stories that we sold in aid of charity, manned stalls at village events promoting the group, and we created stories as a marketing tool to hand out at doctor's surgeries for patients to read while waiting for appointments. After this initial success, we found we wanted different things from our writing, and I moved on. For well over a decade after that, I met more and more local writers at events and writing groups and, over consecutive years, even gave talks at the same book festival I was warned from in the early days. I gained confidence in my writing, and helped to create more fundraising anthologies for various local, regional, and national charities.

I went on to lead and organise writing group events and create a few more, too. Before the pandemic, I was running two community writing groups, a podcast, and a community radio show on creative writing, all alongside running my business and writing books. Since the pandemic, I have streamlined my workload by continuing with the business, writing my own books, running one community group kindly supported by *Society of Authors* and *Essex Libraries*, and recording the podcast.

Finding those who share your interests, kindred spirits you might say, can be difficult at first, but they are there if you look. I learned about creative writing by doing, discovering techniques organically and, later, by visiting the library to research different topics that interested me. While so many of us writers prefer to be introverted, sitting alone with our notebook and pens or in front of the computer, it is worth getting out there and meeting local writers who share the same passions as us. And now, when it behaves itself, social media lends itself as a perfect first or next step to finding those people, your people.

By using hashtags on social media, you will discover a huge resource for writers. #WritingCommunity is one such filter on Twitter/X and Instagram, other platforms too, no doubt. Finding your people is an important step in your own creative journey. While we might choose to work on our stories alone, at some point an urge to speak to someone who understands our literary loves is experienced. Whether that is about a book you both enjoy, or about the writing itself and the methods, techniques, and genres we each employ, conversing with other writers becomes a necessity. That is the content of this book. Moving through some of the basics of creative writing towards more advanced aspects, and with a whole heap of experiences, anecdotes, and tips throughout. It will become a place worth visiting and revisiting during future writing projects.

And, for what it's worth, there is no such thing as a silly question.

Take Away Tips from This Chapter

- Be proactive.
- Create time to write within your schedule.
- Find your people.
- Indulge in conversations with other writers.
- Widen your network.

Chapter 2

Handwriting

Handwriting holds a certain appeal. The sheer act of writing every letter of every word is a blessing. Seeing letters take shape beneath your pen and watching them birth onto your page is a powerful feeling. You created that. Keeping in mind that our alphabet has just twenty-six letters but using them in a multitude of different orders has created centuries of literature that has the capacity to transport readers to other worlds, educate us to doctorate level and beyond, and inform us about the planet upon which we live. It is utterly astounding.

Graphology, that is the study and analysis of handwriting, can give hints about the writer's condition. The pressure the pen applied to the page, twinned with the speed at which letters were written down, gives hints to how rushed, scared, angry, or content the writer was when they wrote it. It also includes clues as to their mood, situation and environment, even their personality. Large loops above or below the line indicate creativity and confidence, and pointed, sharper letters can suggest anger or aggression. Handwriting reflects the writer's daily stresses, giving the reader an insight into their life.

The style of writing we adopt is an individual trait and will probably change throughout our lives. It can alter from our mood, the situation in which we find ourselves, and even our health plays a part. If you think back to your writing in your school books, you'll be assured it probably looks nothing like your handwriting today. Our style of handwriting can change with our mood, our circumstances, our time available for writing, and even adopting fashionable trends. Two examples of this last part are using, or not using, punctuation, or drawing a circle, 'x', or even love heart in place of a dot above the letters 'i' and 'j'. These fashions often fade over time, being replaced with the originally taught dot, or even leaving the space free of any marks at all.

Those curves and spikes we create when forcing the words from our brains through the pen and onto the page become tiny pieces of artwork that hint at our identity. And, if you don't want to form that kind of emotional relationship with letters and words, just think of your writing as another tool, another resource to help you communicate with other people.

Writing by hand, that is writing letters using paper, pen, and envelope, engenders a feeling of nostalgia. It is a much more human approach than is usual nowadays and is a very tactile pursuit. For some, it reminds us of our teenage years when we would send notes to each other in class often when we ought to be focusing on our schoolwork, and for others, it conjures memories of birthday cards from grandparents, thank you notes back to them, or postcards from holiday friendships.

When was the last time you picked up a pen and notebook to write? What was it about choosing a pen and paper that drew you in? Was it your first choice or were you in a hurry to get the words written down? Perhaps it was a note left for someone else, or an aide-memoire like a shopping list? It might have been a telephone message left for a colleague. Whatever the reason you wrote by hand, your first choice was to handwrite it.

Understandably, not everyone likes to work this way. Some people find it difficult to write. Perhaps you have low confidence with your spelling, or you don't really understand what nouns, verbs, or metaphors are, or how they work? Perhaps you just prefer the speed of the computer? Perhaps English is not your first language but you want to write a book or create a writing-related project as a gift for someone? Whatever your reasons, starting a relationship with handwriting may give you a helping hand.

Using a computer to write has become normalised. While I am clearly an advocate for handwriting, I am not averse to using a computer as the benefits are abundantly clear. I have used a computer to write since the 1980s for report writing, letters, and memos. My own writing, that is the stories, poems, and diary entries I created since my teenage years were almost always handwritten in notebooks. Nowadays, as a professional writer and novelist, I use a laptop. The reasons for this are many, not least because of the speed at which I can write a lengthy piece, the ease of editing it, and a computer will have instant access to the internet, which allows me to send the resulting piece via e-mail. From a professional point of view, if I handwrote everything instead of using the laptop, and posted my novels and non-fiction through the post, my daily job would be hindered by impracticalities.

Writing by hand need not be considered a memory. While handwriting may be less utilised today, it is still a useful skill. Of course, handwriting can slow us down when we want to get our points written quickly and slow our thought processes and writing speed. Yet the slow speed we experience when we handwrite allows us to take that moment to think about the topic a little clearer. By forcing us to slow down, we are engaging with our minds that little bit more. When, in today's world, rushing seems the natural thing to do, handwriting forces us to take just a moment longer.

Tip: Try using a pen and pad when you need to think about your choice of words. Writing individual letters stops us rushing to the next thing and forces us to take a moment.

Relying on your fingers, pen, and brain to work in unison can be magical if you think about it, and your handwriting can show your own style and identity. However, I still use a notebook and pen when I am outlining a story or fleshing out a character's looks and their motivations before transferring the findings to the computer. I believe this is for two reasons: firstly, that using a pen and pad is very much part of my own personal writing process, so I can feel the words beneath the pen and see them forming into whatever I am trying to express. Secondly, because gathering my thoughts onto paper creates a tactile environment that helps with the thinking and generating of ideas.

When it comes to trying the writing exercises I recommend later within this book, please do them in whatever way makes you happy and whatever achieves the best results for the writing project because no one size fits all. Try them different ways, with paper and pen, on a laptop, on a tablet, maybe with colourful charts and graphs. Whether writing by hand or typing upon a keyboard works better for you, you do you because using a method that does not feel right will probably make you change your mind about trying it at all. For those of us who are drawn to colourful stationery, perhaps adapt the exercises by using highlighter markers, or sticky pads. The point is to use the exercises in a way that you enjoy, and that achieves a good result because while this book will guide you with creative writing, if enjoyment is a major part of the project, you will be more likely to stick with it until it is finished.

Take Away Tips from this Chapter

- Graphology can be fascinating.
- Experiment with different writing styles to find your favourite.
- Form a positive relationship with handwriting.
- Learn to love those curves and spikes.
- Try different styles of handwriting that better reflect you today.

Chapter 3

Simple Creative Writing Projects

T here are so many creative writing project ideas out there, and best of all most of them can be adapted to fit our own requirements. I have found that when we are just starting out on a project, trying something simple is a good idea. I believe this is because if we try something simple and achieve it, then it gives us the confidence to try something bigger and better afterwards. And all it takes is that have-a-go attitude and a tiny bit of confidence in the first place. Of course, a little curiosity will help. A curious mind can be a marvellous ingredient to add to this creative mix.

Writing Regularly

It is said that if you do something regularly, it becomes part of your routine. Therefore, if you write every day, it will become so habitual that you won't look for reasons not to write, in fact you may begin looking forward to it. You can massively help yourself by writing at the same time each day, so your mind and body become used to the routine. Including fun things within your daily schedule means you will miss them if you don't do them. Nobody likes to miss things they consider fun or a good use of their time, so writing every day can be a good habit to adopt.

Perhaps consider writing upon waking or during your tea break when your mind is active and ready to respond. If you are writing a novel during lunchtime at work, each work day you will be thinking about the novel as lunchtime approaches. If you find you have more time to yourself during a specific time each week, you will find it easier to keep writing within your schedule.

Letter Writing

Most people use computers to communicate nowadays, but there is a section of society that still loves to write by hand. I am very much one of them. Ask most people today and they'll tell you e-mailing is their preferred method of communication. Of course, it has its plus points: it is instant, easy, and you don't need a postage stamp. However, much of today's correspondence can lack that human touch that a letter can bring. That's not to suggest electronic mail doesn't have its place, it very much does, but allowing tone, mood, and even humour to be exhibited through your written words is surely a more treasured way to correspond every so often. After all, how many times have you found an email was too pushy, abrupt, or even rude? Emojis are useful only to a point.

Back when letter writing was the only means of communication, and we didn't rely on phoning or texting each other or using social media apps, we relied on handwriting not only to keep in touch with friends and family, but also to apply for employment, requesting hands in marriage and register births, deaths, and marriages.

You will find that letter writing is a particularly tactile pursuit. I've been writing letters to friends since my teenage years in the 1980s. Because I enjoy handwriting so much, and receiving handwritten letters, I've managed to accumulate around half a dozen penfriends at any one time. Since 2019, I have organised most of my recent letters in a box so I can re-read them at my leisure. It is a handy exercise reminding me to revisit them before I write back with answers to their questions. If you read them in date order, you would discover a conversation of sorts that includes a social context.

The box also contains letters from those no longer with us, so have become tiny time capsules of the senders' personalities. They remain an example of their handwriting, personal word choice that was usual from them, and of course evokes wonderful memories that can never be taken away. They are a tactile reminder of our connections and relationships.

During the start of the pandemic and the ensuing lockdown within the UK, there was a huge sense of connection when a handwritten letter was received. Often these letters included the writer's fear and anxiety of the worldwide situation, which was shared by many, and as such contents became a social record. There was even a drive for people to handwrite letters to the elderly in care homes given that relatives were not permitted to visit. It gave the recipients someone to chat with through the medium of letters and words. Seeing a handwritten letter in your letter box always fills the recipient with curiosity, so give them something extra to be excited about. Realistically, handwritten letters are unlikely to become a regular part of our lives again, however in a book about creative writing, you could consider writing them a project between friends and keep an age-old tradition alive at the same time.

Here are a few of ideas to stimulate your letter writing:

- Use attractive writing paper that will show your personality, or just be a pleasure for you to write upon.

- Use pages from a notebook that you will have to tear from the spine. Tearing the pages from a spiral-bound, hard-backed notebook is a particularly satisfying sound.
- Use a good, sturdy pen that sits comfortably between your fingers and glides smoothly across the page. Anything scratchy on the paper or cumbersome in your hand will likely result in discontinuing this activity.
- Use letter writing as a practical exercise to remind you what your handwriting looks like. Most people's writing changes over the years. What was yours like when you were a child at school and what is it like now?
- If you include a photograph inside the letter, do ensure you get the envelope weighed at the post office. If you rely on guessing its cost, your tiny treasure may end up lost on its journey.
- The effort you put into the letter will undoubtedly be welcomed at its destination. Consider your own feelings when a handwritten letter arrives through your door. Curiosity over the contents is likely to be your first feeling, with excitement a close second.
- Ensure your writing can be read. We might rush words if we are in a hurry or even when we are excited to get the words down but remember that the person receiving the letter doesn't know what you intended to write. Aside from rushed writing leading to misshapen letters and words resulting in confusion for the reader, rushed writing also implies you didn't have time to write, so find a time when you are able to write clearly.

What to Include

One of the best things about writing letters to friends or family is that we have to give thought to the words we use because the letter, somehow, feels more personal than an e-mail. Our choice of subject topics may be different too from person to person, generation to generation, and location. There are so many topics to include aside from the usual enquiries of health and weather. Why not raise questions on daily and family news, events you will or intend to attend, mini reviews on books you are reading or movies you watched. Raising questions gives a feeling to the recipient of responding with the answer. If letters contain statements of what you have done rather than raising questions, there is nothing for the recipient to respond with aside from the good mannered 'ah, that's nice' reaction. While there is nothing wrong with this, a back-and-forth method is much more interesting to both parties.

Once sent, and hopefully a response received, why not keep it in a special box as mentioned earlier? If you have several responses, you could keep them together or have separate compartments for each person's letter. I have always intended to decorate mine into a keepsake box. Because of my feelings surrounding handwriting and postal correspondence, it makes sense to view it this way.

Lastly, when you receive a response from your pen friend, how did it make you feel? Were you excited when you saw it come through the letterbox? Were you curious or cautious to read its contents? Does that curiosity or caution relate to the person it was from or from the topics you wrote about originally? Did you feel special knowing someone had taken the time to write to you the same way?

Daily Diary

Diaries are written for oneself and are a space to collect your personal thoughts. Although not all diaries will be used in this straightforward way, some will. When we mention a diary, some people will instantly consider a video diary. While mostly technological, some creators will write themselves a script that acts as a prompt before and during filming. Video diaries are quick and easy to create thanks to the technology we have at our fingertips, and fun to create as well. If we view them analytically, they are a superb record of societal and cultural aspects of our modern world, because through them we discover everything from today's fashion, rhetoric, culture, art, architecture, etc.

However, in a book about creative writing, let's look at physical diaries. For centuries it was quite the thing to write your thoughts, hopes, intentions, even your secrets in a book. Poets and writers relied upon diaries to record their thoughts and keep notes on observations they wanted to include in their next poem or story.

While diaries have never really gone out of fashion, there are only a handful of people who tell me they write regularly in one. During our lives, some of us find a reason to keep a diary even if for a limited amount of time or for a specific reason. Maybe we use it to record our everyday feelings while on holiday, or to help us get over a break-up. As touched upon briefly, some use diaries to record their dreams upon waking while they are still fresh in our minds.

While diaries are great to keep for everyday use, they are also great to revisit our views. Some people even have multi-use diaries that provide dates and times as well as spaces for notes to be used within your novel writing.

Diaries can also have a profound effect on us, aside from the everyday companion. Some years ago, as a way of helping us process a family emergency, we were urged by the hospital to write in a diary. It was intended for us all to use. These collective entries behaved both as an aide-memoire for the patient when they were eventually discharged, and for us to continue processing what had happened. As they were released within a week, we had just a few days' worth of entries, but the time they missed while being unwell meant they had blank spaces in their memory to fill. As far as they were concerned, they went to bed one day and awoke in hospital another. Reading the diary helped to fill in those blanks as well as understand how serious their condition was. It also reminded them how treasured they were learning this through our choice of emotional and profound words as none of us knew if they would ever recover. This way, a diary can be used as a processing and recovery resource for the convalescing patient.

Most diaries are not intended to be read by other people. They are a private conversation between the writer and the diary itself. The book becomes a kind of confidante. Some diaries even come with a lock and key attached that reinforces this point. This confidentiality falls apart, however, when diaries become books that can be read by anyone. I mention this because when I was at university as a mature student just a few years ago, one of our assignments was to give critical thought to the contents of several different diaries written back in the nineteenth century. They were based around the topics of literature, religion, and politics. From the content, it was clear at least one of the writers had had no intention of others reading the work. While diaries are intended to be private, respect of that privacy must come into the equation, too.

Many a story written as a book has been set upon the theme of a diary or had one used as a plot device. Some have become particularly noteworthy too and have become political, historical, and social records, such as *The Diary of Anne Frank* and those by seventeenth-century diarist Samuel Pepys. Ironically, despite highlighting the confidentiality issues mentioned above, many are intended to be consumed by an audience rather than simply standing as a conversation between the diary and the author. Even fictional diaries have come to the forefront of popular culture, including *The Secret Diary of Adrian Mole Aged 13¾* by Sue Townsend, or adapted from books into movies, like *Bridget Jones' Diary* by Helen Fielding, and that of the diary of Tom Riddle within *Harry Potter and the Half Blood Prince* by J.K. Rowling.

Should you use a diary yourself to record your everyday life and that of the world surrounding you, you could consider this a creative writing project because, chances are, you are probably writing it by hand and if it is a physical book it may lend itself to be embellished, which could be another creative project. Should you be typing the diary into your computer, you can keep its contents as private as you like because the document will have a facility to create a password, and so password-protecting your diary may be a useful security measure for your project.

In a recent clear out, I discovered a few of my own old diaries. One was from my childhood and within it were entries of a family holiday and the adventures I got up to. It had not been written in regularly but highlights itself as an example of my terrible childlike handwriting with bored-easily scribbles out, and even simplistic sketches. It is a miniature time capsule and after a quick re-read (there were not enough entries for anything longer), I discovered I even remembered the holiday I was on when I wrote it.

Another diary was from my thirties. It was filled with thoughts and feelings of the day, and my thoughts of films I had watched. These were essentially mini movie reviews. I also recorded my dreams here. One particular diary was thick with a navy blue hardback cover. I remember writing in it every night. The writing style generally echoed my feelings: scruffy showing I was short of patience and hurrying to get the gist down. In some entries I wrote for several pages, not impatient to write but quick to move the pen so much that my words (not word choice) got larger and stretched lengthways and widthways until they took up the space of two or three lines. You can read the words, but more could have been said if I had used the book as it was designed to be used.

These diaries were used for years to record daily life and thoughts, secrets, and most often dreams I had the night before. I never wrote them to be read by other eyes, of this I was certain, yet at the same time I used special methods of security so nobody would understand the words. For example, I used initials or code names in place of real names in case my thoughts and secrets were discovered. Now I realise those details were and are of no interest to other people. Not even a tiny bit! I even used a kind of shorthand whereby I would refer to actors with their initials rather than their name, though I don't recall if that was because I was writing so fast that I just did not have time or intention to write their name in full, or if I just didn't want anyone to know who I was talking about. That said, so incredibly security conscious was I that I taped in pictures of the actors from magazines, so if writing their initials was to hide their identity, I did a very poor job!

These diaries serve as a snapshot of my life and thought process, as well as a resource for countless writing prompts should I ever create a story about life back then. Fashions were mentioned as well as music, movies, celebrities, books, work life, friends, family, and pets. I had no idea I would keep these miniature time capsules, but I treasure them.

It is easy to get blurry eyed over possessions from the past, but it is also best not to get too nostalgic over everything you ever owned, because that can easily turn into a hoarding issue where nothing is destroyed or recycled.

What to Include

I have highlighted several diary topics above but write whatever you like, especially if it is intended to remain a record between you and the diary. While topics mentioned here have included medical records, holiday memories, movie reviews, and dream recording, some people use diaries to record ideas for stories. Whether writing the initial notes for a story or using the diary to keep records of its progression from the initial inspiration through to the creation of characters and plot, be sure to write the date. It may stand as evidence to prove your ownership of the story should it come to it. Legalities aside, using a diary to write story notes means you can watch your personal progress developing. Having a summary in diary form can be a useful writing progress aid for you to look back and see how the story began, and as a guide to gauge against other story progressions.

Journaling

While the contents of journaling overlap with keeping a diary, journals have other uses, too. Journaling can be less personal than a diary incorporating notes and observations from life in the outside world than inside your mind. Journals are usually written to be published, whereas diaries are often intended to be kept private. Of course, a journal requires a journalist to write it. Later you will read how aspects of detective work and investigative journalism join forces when you develop a story idea. It helps to have a curious mind when taking to creative writing of any kind.

Calligraphy

Calligraphy lends itself to becoming an instant creative writing project since it is, itself, a purely decorative way to use the alphabet. Calligraphy has roots back in ancient China some two thousand years ago. One might expect to see examples of calligraphy, or decorative writing, in a church, upon hand-bound books in ancient libraries, and even decorative wall hangings. But that is how it is used, learning it is its own project. Calligraphy can be fun to try using ink pots and quills or steel nibs. It has an immense feeling of nostalgia about it, yet also may feel a bit on the fussy side nowadays.

Nevertheless, if you have an opportunity to try it, the feeling of creating elaborate letters with long swooping loops and swirls, especially with different-coloured inks, can create some amazing creative works.

Whether you use it for fun, to decorate the cover of a handwritten book, use it to decorate a legacy project, or you pen a letter to a pen pal using this wildly elaborate method of writing, it is sure to be a hit. Because it is so beautiful, unlike straightforward, everyday handwriting, I believe calligraphy should be a seen as an activity we never stop using or showing interest in.

Take Away Tips from this Chapter

- Start simple.
- Gain confidence with small and simple projects.
- Try calligraphy.
- Keep a diary.
- Start a journal.

Chapter 4

Creative Writing Exercises for All Ages

When we hear the word exercise attached to the thing we enjoy doing, in this case creative writing, it is sometimes met with a little disappointment. Exercise sounds like hard work! It also feels very school-like and pedestrian. However, participating in a writing exercise can be immense fun and strangely fulfilling. Finding or creating them need not be a chore and can be enjoyable. It is really all about making them work for you to get the best out of them.

For generations, writers have used exercises to rustle up their imagination before embarking on a writing project. Mostly we do it when we need help generating ideas or developing aspects of an existing project, or to find inspiration for the initial first sentence. Loosening up our imagination is similar to visiting the gym. You wouldn't begin a gym session without getting your stretches done first, so a few cerebral challenges here and there help us to get the best from our imagination before and during a writing session. But we don't always do it before we begin or continue a project, sometimes we do it just for fun and because we enjoy working with or playing with words.

Adapt to Fit

A trick to making them fun and more accessible to everyone is to adapt them to your individual needs. Often, that brings about the same energy and excitement as the intended writing itself. It's all about finding what works for you and your level of creativity, and what time you have available. You don't always need an exercise to help get your imagination working effectively, but if you try one or two it may become a regular thing, and if it helps the resulting work it's worth your time.

If the exercise is designed to be carried out alone, creating a workable environment will be key. Ensure you have all the equipment you require, whether that is simply your laptop or a pen and pad. Some of us more anxious types will likely prefer several pens rather than the solitary one, just in case you are at a crucial point of hashing out ideas and the pen runs out. So gather as many writing tools you need in order to be comfortable enough to relax and let the words flow.

If the exercise is intended to be enjoyed with others, perhaps around a table, try to arrange it so that everyone is facing each other. This will create the feeling of teamwork, despite the fact you will all be working individually. Seeing the excitement – and competition – in everyone's expressions will help the exercise become successful.

Most writing exercises are developed for adult writers, new or experienced. I note that last part because often it doesn't matter if the writer has experience with writing or not since exercises are created to spark your brain into life. Therefore, it's more about the creativity the writer brings to the table and what they, individually, can get from it. Adapting these exercises for children can be as enjoyable as the exercise itself, and all it takes is a little open-minded imagination.

Below is a selection of writing exercises designed for adults but with a little tinkering and creativity younger writers and children will get something from them, too. I have used most of these myself so appreciate how well they can be adapted to working alone or in groups. They also work well in writing group or writing workshop situations. Depending on the exercise and hoped-for results, they can be used as icebreakers, too.

Tip: If used as an icebreaker keep an eye on quieter writers ensuring they are not overshadowed by the more extrovert ones. Writing exercises ought to be enjoyed by all participants.

Brainstorming

Brainstorming, within the context of storytelling, is about gathering ideas. This is probably the number one go-to writing exercise, and although it may not start out specifically for writing it can certainly help you gather ideas. Using the metaphor of cookery, brainstorming is the creation of interesting and exciting ingredients, after which you can mix them together to create a literary cake. The cherry on the top would be that the story works once it's written. Early stages of a brainstorming session help us consider the basics of story construction upon which we add building blocks from the foundations up.

Brainstorming is a handy resource if you don't yet have ideas to work with, or they need fleshing out for the story to gather momentum. You are not limited with numbers of participants as this is an exercise that will work as well for one person as it can with several. The more people participating in a session, though, the more it may make for a messier outcome. If you are not precious on the type of result, the exercise will at least loosen up the imagination.

My number one piece of advice for idea gathering is to be as open-minded as you possibly can. After the initial gathering of ideas, glue them together to form a cohesive and exciting plot. Cohesion and excitement do need to work together in this case because the cohesion allows it all to work logically, and if the idea excites you then you are more likely to write the story. Take it in turns to come up with a character gender, name, a genre, a goal, and a location or setting, taking each in turn, ensuring you don't move to the next person without first completing their go. Ensure someone jots down each of the answers. Once you have gone around the table and everyone has had a go, start again. This should help you gather a workable plot that can be continually fleshed out until you have enough notes to start writing. At this stage, do not be afraid of going off on a tangent. Sometimes tangents are better than the original idea, so don't fight them if they are workable.

Speaking of tangents, they can be useful and they can be a waste of time, but you won't know which until you have investigated them. Perhaps you will take some of one tangent and part of another to create your story? Ensure someone jots down all the ideas so you can revisit them once the session is over.

Tip: Don't be afraid to say your findings out loud as well as jotting them down, even if you are doing this exercise alone. Not enough credit is given to those writers who talk to themselves. Doing so can help you create a better result.

Here's a simple example, but you can create your own:

- Gender: Woman
- Genre: Action
- Goal: To rescue her husband from peril

Don't be too concerned at this stage if the idea feels trite or overdone. What you are trying to do is create a foundation to work with. There is nothing to say that foundation will change in part or completely. What may begin as a potentially overdone story often branches out in many different areas, gathers sub-genres and even blends genres, so just allow the ideas to come. Along the way you can change or alter the gender, goal, and genre, even creating your own because world building can very much be part of this initial process, but try not to get too caught up in the finer details at this stage. There will be plenty of time to investigate your characters and their goals during story development. The final story may even be totally unconnected with the one you brainstormed, but if any potentially workable ideas came out of the session, why not jot them down to revisit another time?

Tip: Just because genres are fixed categories does not mean you cannot create your own.

Keep it simple at the start until you are sure the story is exciting to you. At these early stages, you can give thought to the character's name, appearance, the location of the story, the era, etc. Check out Chapter 5: Writing Fiction, which covers story development in detail. A plot may be forming at this stage, but if it doesn't that is not a problem. It just means you need to continue brainstorming until something excites you and a plot is born. Your characters may change gender throughout this exercise, backstories, even goals. Your plot could change, too. There will become a time during this exercise that, with all the findings gathered, you are excited enough with the idea you found and set your mind to writing it.

Tip: Add more tension to the whole exercise by adding a timer.

Free Writing

A free write is exactly what it claims: writing freely. Depending on your reasons for free writing, you can add parameters like a timer or a genre. Although there may be more, I see free writes as good for two distinct things: for exercising your imagination muscles before a bigger writing session much like warming up before jogging, and secondly as a method to empty your mind of all the stuff stopping you writing.

Free writing can be absolutely anything from whatever just angered you, a shopping list, a recap of a conversation, something you want to discuss with your partner, a list of the chores you want to complete before the end of the week, a review of a movie that stayed in your mind, a review of an actor in your favourite TV show, your thoughts behind a radio show call-in, last night's dream, a childhood memory, an idea of a story you want to expand, a poem, absolutely anything at all.

Timed Free Writing

This exercise is the same as a free write except you do it with a timer on. The idea of that might freak some writers out to the point that they avoid any timed session at all. On the other hand, having a timer switched on helps you focus on your mind and gives you the motivation and incentive to get something written. This can be especially useful if you are plagued by distractions. It is also a really good method of writing under self-imposed pressure. Writing on demand (and focusing on demand) are good skills throughout life.

There is no specific amount of time to use, just whatever you think will work for your situation. Try the exercise a few different ways, perhaps beginning with a five-minute session, then a ten-minute. Fifteen-, twenty-, thirty, and sixty-minute sessions are really helpful for when planning a larger story.

Timers are helpful to those writers who find themselves becoming distracted easily, especially if your mobile phone beeps or vibrates a notification. Even for general writing sessions, like writing this book, I used a timer for thirty- and sixty-minute bursts.

Prompted Free Writing

As you might imagine, a prompted free write employs a prompt by way of giving your mind some stimulation. It may sound like an oxymoron to give yourself boundaries during a free write, but all these suggestions can really help motivate you.

Prompts can be anything from a line of text, a physical item, music, anything. Music is a great prompt but if lyrics are likely to disturb your writing flow, perhaps something lyric-free may be the answer for you. Although don't assume that is the case for every time you write. Our moods are as different as our music tastes. It is worth noting, too, that choosing a piece of music that doesn't necessarily sit smoothly within your usual musical taste could be a good idea. These tiny adjustments in our tastes can jolt our mind into exploring ideas we might never have given time or thought to before. Be creative with your music prompts and see where they take you.

Just as sound or music prompts can activate your imagination, so can word or sentence prompts. There are several ways you can put this into action: choosing a book from your shelf and opening it at a random page, then looking at an equally random sentence. Use that and go from there. Alternatively, close your eyes when you pick up the book and choose the page and sentence for this exercise to be truly freeing. Another method would be to flick through a dictionary and use the first word you see.

Lastly, though there are doubtless more ways, gather a list of words that you find yourself drawn to. Do this over time. Have the list accessible, perhaps stuck to your notebook or an easily found document on your laptop, and simply tick off the next word to be used. Because a prompted free write lends itself to being incredibly random, there is a good chance you can put this skill to good use by writing on demand whenever you need or want to. Skills like this are great in all aspects of life. If you are limited for time, being able to just open your notebook, grab a word from the air, and write something is a wonder and a blessing all wrapped up in one.

Tip: Giving your mind something creative to focus on helps the time move by and produces a piece of work that can be edited later. I used this technique when I needed to get my mind off something unpleasant, like waiting for a flight (I don't like airports or planes). You can use this exercise on the flight as well.

Prompt

As mentioned, prompts vary from person to person. What suits one writer will not suit another, so you are the best person to know what will prompt your imagination. Examples of prompts I have used in the past are music, photographs, and physical items, etc.

Music can be an excellent writing prompt and has as many diverse genres as literature. If the lyrics of a song gets you into the mood for thinking about the story it tells, maybe that is all you will need. Some of us are drawn to classical music, some to rock, others to country or pop, or synthesised music, or movie scores. Whatever will provide that background atmosphere for you and get you to create something readable is what you want.

Photographic prompts are one of my favourite resources. Because I am a keen amateur photographer, I generally have a camera on me all the time. If I see something that looks interesting, I will add it to my vast photographic library. Photographic prompts are especially helpful of all the prompts I have used because if you study the picture, you get something quite different from it. For example, the picture can act as a metaphor, or you may ask of the subject questions, or perhaps the black and white photo in your local café holds special meaning to you. Perhaps the colour photo you just captured instantly tells the story of all life. It is now up to you to transfer that story onto the page. You can glean more information from *Writing Naked: Writing Without Boundaries*, written to highlight word and pictorial prompts.

Physical items are great as writing prompts. Random items from around the house are often the best kind to work with. These are the items that hide in plain sight, that you tend not to notice because you stare at them every day. These are the items that, perhaps, hold more stories because they see everyday life happen around them. Do you ever wonder what they see or hear that you didn't? Of course, we have to suspend belief momentarily by imagining that the kettle can see or hear you, or that the washing machine is watching you, but with a little imagination these everyday inanimate objects could have such stories to tell!

Objects that are less hidden yet still intriguing are also good to use. The half-filled bottle of sparkly blue nail polish kept on the mantelpiece might tell of the night it socialised in all its glory, the mug with 'Best Mum' emblazoned on the side is sad because it is not used much nowadays, and the scarlet lipstick in the draw that nobody ever used but is never thrown away questions why it was purchased in the first place – all these items have a story attached. And it is up to you as the writer to investigate that story and write it. A prompted free write is the great place to do that.

Consider using fragrance and fabrics as prompts as well. Fragrances are well known for evoking memories, and the touch of different fabrics help us feel more, which will show in the choice of words we use when writing.

Word Prompts

Detritus
Acerbic
Determined
Ancestor
Cantilever
Professional
Delinquent
Overwhelmed
Undermined
Overlooked

Sentence Prompts

- Dark rooms always brought out the worst in her.
- The colours were magical, as if I hadn't lost my sight at all.
- She ran her hand over the satin fabric. This wedding was going to be better than all the others, and in so many ways, too.
- As she walked up the path, the lavender's scent took her back decades.
- Strawberries always were his favourite. A touch of gravy over them completed the dish.
- The wind rushed over his face, sending tiny water droplets that fell from the sails over his cheeks.
- Time was running out. Red wire or green? A decision needed to be made.
- The scene in front told her all she needed to know.
- Finally in place, the scaffolding was up. Stopping the house falling was just one item on a never-ending list for this restoration project.
- He held the mobile phone to his ear as traffic rushed by, bringing with it debris from the carriageway.

Reading

For many of us, reading is a pastime. For others it is a link to the outside world. There are those readers who consume books quicker than the author can write them, and those more occasional readers who enjoy books now and again.

While entertainment and escapism are often the end result for most, for writers reading can help hone our skills. Observing how other writers use their voice, form a style, and knit together sentences to form paragraphs and chapters will help you understand how to form your own. If you analyse and critically read other writers' books with an eye to learning you will gather ideas for yourself.

Writing Challenges

I see the words 'Writing Challenges' in two ways: there are those challenges within our writing where we get caught or write ourselves into a corner, and there are those challenges in which we participate. The former is dealt with in Chapter 9: Troubleshooting. The latter are usually found online and there is an abundance if you know where to look.

One of them, possibly the biggest, is called NaNoWriMo and stands for National Novel Writing Month (www.nanowrimo.org), which takes place in November. It is especially useful for those writers who have a story in mind but no time to write, trouble focusing attention, or problems seeing projects through to the end. It is also excellent for those writers who have been on the same manuscript for years, tinkering with it, attempting to perfect it here and there, editing it to within an inch of its life, or wondering and worrying what other people will think of it. Have you ever heard someone say they have a book in them, but then they never do anything about it? If so, NaNoWriMo is definitely for all these types of writers.

NaNoWriMo somehow forces us to get the job done. I suspect the reason is because the challenge is all about the date. Thirty days is thirty days, but then it is also just thirty days. The idea behind the challenge is to instil habitual writing, creating a daily routine. Throughout November you write every day at least 1,667 words to get to the last day, resulting in fifty thousand words. This amount of words provides the foundation of a novel. However, over the years, the challenge has evolved into more of a worldwide community of writers who use it to begin or complete their Work in Progress (WiP). Those who have a tough time finding a moment to write use this challenge to gain momentum with their novel.

There are other ways to approach NaNoWriMo, too. There is a section on the site for 'Rebels'. This is a place where I often found a home. Rebels are invited to NaNoWriMo their way through November by completing whichever writing project they want. When I participated in this part, I had ideas for stories but none of them were novel length, therefore I decided to write thirty days' worth of short stories. Thus, I was still participating but I was not writing a specific novel. This was a better challenge for me at the time and in preparation for it I had written a list of thirty individual word prompts and intended to use one each day. It did not matter if any story was shorter than the daily word count of 1,667 because while some of mine were around one thousand words, I had several stories of approximately seven thousand words, so I had more than made up for the word count. What ended up as heaps of short stories provided me with ideas upon which to develop. Some of these are, indeed, novel-worthy, but some are complete in their shorter format.

If you are writing a novel, by the end of November you will have completed fifty thousand words of it, producing, possibly, its backbone. From there you can put flesh on those bones and develop the story, create depth for the characters, and focus more on creative writing techniques and devices.

NaNoWriMo is a great writers' resource (as well as challenge) but its set-up won't be for everyone. When participating, we put a fair amount of pressure on ourselves and when you consider that November is just before the festive season for some, it does tend to challenge you in other ways. Finding time to write around two thousand words every single day without fail is a major challenge, too. My biggest piece of advice would be to prepare and have a supportive network because there will be days you cannot join in with family activities because the writing must come first if you are to complete the challenge.

I touched upon the community aspect of NaNoWriMo earlier. This is by far one of its best resources. Through the website, you can connect with other writers in your area through your 'Municipal Liaison'. This person will arrange local 'Write-Ins' that you can join. Some of these may take place in a library, a coffee shop, a book shop, a pub, just about anywhere a community group can spend time. This in turn aids the local economy, which is never a bad thing. During these Write-Ins, you can bring along your laptop or pen and pad and use the time to write. There may be a schedule in place where a break in writing occurs and everyone can introduce themselves, or that may happen at the beginning. The essence of each Write-In is to write, not chat. Many people bring earphones to help them focus and others simply use the time to research their topic, therefore library Write-Ins are particularly useful for this.

Upon the NaNoWriMo website, there is an area where you can gauge your progress. This is the part that most writers will be checking daily – sometimes hourly! It will also show you the progress of other writers you have connected with and serves as a reminder that NaNoWriMo is not a competition, it is a challenge.

I completed NaNoWriMo for eight consecutive years. Of those years I managed to write four novels and several short stories, accumulating enough material to keep me occupied for years to come.

Tip: When participating, use the first week to create a huge word count buffer. When you begin to lull in the next week or two, this buffer will come into its own.

If the penultimate month of the year is too busy for your lifestyle, why not instead join Camp Nano, which takes place in April and July. Discover more information from www.nanowrimo.org.

Other challenges include those within *Writing Magazine*. A fabulous writers' resource, this paper and online magazine provides a plethora of information, advice, services, competitions, and challenges. It is a great resource for writers, in whichever stage they find themselves. For local writing challenges, perhaps seek out your community's writing group either online or via your local library. For more information on writing groups within this guide, check out Chapter 5: Writing Fiction.

Clothing

Rather an elaborate exercise, but it works for some writers. If you dress in the clothing a character would use, it can help alter your mood, environment, and atmosphere to write more in line with them. If it is a character another author has made up, chances are you can probably hire some clothes for the exercise, although it can be much more fun and in keeping with the creativity of it all to make or fumble together their clothing from anything you have at home.

Physical Item

People love to handle these items because physical touch can give us so much information to use. Physical items engender the urge to touch and, usually, the writer's first thought is to want to pick it up and handle it. This is great news. The more curious a mind, potentially the better the outcome.

Sensory activities aid curiosity and help feed the imagination. An open mind fuels curiosity. It is during these sessions that adults can take on the curiosity of children by asking the items questions. Why? Where? How? Who? When?

This method is one I use regularly when I hold creative writing courses. Gather a selection of random items from your travels or even from around the house. Put them in the centre of a table and gather your writers around the table. Either have your writers close their eyes and pick one or simply choose the one they like the best. Once they hold the item, have them look it over. Every inch of it. Feel it, smell it, shake it, listen to it, even taste it if that's appropriate. Using these senses can give us a different view of the item than we would ordinarily.

One of the items I have in my collection is a bottle of blue, sparkly nail polish. I would have the writer pick up the bottle, shake it, watching the sparkles do their thing. If appropriate, I would have them open the bottle smell the liquid, which can be pungent, perhaps even use a little on their nail so they can see how it smooths itself out. Have them write five lines of description of their experiences carrying out the research. Once they have completed them, perhaps write a story of approximately one hundred words. Have them consider its backstory using questions like:

- Where were you before you came here?
- Who created you?
- Why did they create you?

- Why are you this colour?
- Tell me about the person who created you.

Others items I keep are a Christmas decoration, a book about eighty years old bought from a charity shop that has a handwritten message inside, and a roll of photographic film still within its plastic lidded tub. Each of these items yield a plethora of questions.

Word Jar

This is an interesting exercise and, because it is quite visual, younger children might want to join in. Repurpose a glass jar that maybe once was home to something like coffee granules. The jar ought to have a lid and be transparent, so wash away the label. Keep it somewhere seen, perhaps near the television or dinner table, so nobody forgets to use it. Write on a scrap of paper something good that happened to you, something good you heard, an interesting fact that made you smile, and pop in into the jar. For younger children write a single word on the paper, perhaps an action like a smile, or running, or a colour. For added visual interest, you could use scraps of coloured paper but do ensure that everyone uses different colours so you cannot instantly identify that all the yellow pieces were from John, all the white pieces were from Alex, and all the red pieces were from Jenny. Seeing the papers increase inside the jar adds to the anticipation of what might be included.

Mix them up and by the end of the week there should be plenty of pieces of paper inside the jar. When it is time to open the jar, ensure each participant takes a piece of paper – even if it is their own – and when everyone has taken one, each person takes another until all the pieces are chosen. Each player must not share their 'stash'. The exercise is to form a short story from every comment they received, even if they identify their own. For younger children who may need help piecing together a story, perhaps invite them to act it out and someone else write it. Allow a set amount of time to write the story.

Tip 1: Read your story aloud at the end, identifying the genre, the main character, and the plot afterwards. Allow everyone to offer their opinion of the genre, main character, and plot to ensure it is clear cut.
Tip 2: Pass your story to your neighbour to read aloud, adhering to the suggestion in Tip 1 above.

Perhaps organise a prize for the best story.

An Alphabetical Story

This exercise focuses the mind on making up a story using every letter of the alphabet in order. Try to keep with a theme, if possible. An example might be: Angela baked cakes, delivering endless fancies. Gillian had implied John's kids liked meringues, not oranges. Preferring quiches, Robert squashed tartlets under very wild X-rays. Yes! Zany.

As you can see, it is quite a challenge already, but if you want an extra challenge set a timer!

Writing Activities for Younger Folk

As previously mentioned, most writing activities are for adults. However, we do need a new generation of writers to fill our seats once ours have vacated, so what better time to get younger people interested in writing and publishing?

Children have the best imaginations with fewer filters or inhibitions so, technically, they could produce the ultimate in amazing stories because they are from the freshest minds. However, children rely less on logic and more on fantasy to make a story work. If we help them focus on keeping that childlike quality of not worrying if they mess up, they can learn a lot more.

Framing the Idea

A good result usually works when it has been framed in a fun way. Saying to an eight-year-old, 'let's do some writing exercises,' will probably be met with misery as images of their teachers and classroom activities will fill their minds. And who wants to work in their downtime? Children have plenty of writing exercises through their school curriculum, so having a child agree to participate in a writing exercise will need some careful framing.

Games and fun activities get the best results if the child is surrounded by other children, unless your child works better alone. After-school meet-ups, children's birthday parties, and sleepovers are all good occasions to organise some of these games. How the child fares at school and their feelings towards writing will determine whether you may need to reframe the idea, and much depends on their age and ability. Parental or guardian discretion is recommended when organising your young scribes.

Framing the suggestion with something like, 'At your sleepover, we can do all kinds of games. You're good with spellings, so why don't we have a word game too?' Highlighting one of their strengths can instantly get their competitive side glowing, so they cannot wait to show off to their friends.

Secretly Learning

If your child somehow repels the idea of learning because it may have been forced down their throat, here is a helpful, if somewhat sneaky, teaching aid. Do you remember how your mother used to hide the peas and carrots inside the shepherd's pie when you were little, just so you would eat it all? Or perhaps if they made their own bread, they used the water the veggies were cooked in so the nutrients were hidden inside the bread? Hiding obvious education within fun games is the same kind of sneaky teaching I am highlighting here. At the end of the game, they learned through enjoyment without realising they did.

If the words 'sneaky' and 'secret' bother you, reframe them with the word 'creative' instead. Creative writing isn't just about making up stories, it is also about word choice and the power of words.

You might be amazed at how weighty words can be when they reframe an idea, product, or service that will eventually find a happy home inside your mind – and even make you part with the contents of your wallet.

The skills children learn through creative writing are many and can certainly help their confidence in expression. Exercises on words and widening vocabulary are a blessing. A child with a healthy love of words will find this skill will be of immense help to them in life.

Long Word List

Years ago, when my daughter was in primary school, during our walk home we would chat about what she had done in class. One day the class had been painting butterflies, that is painting one side of a butterfly on a piece of paper, folding the page together and seeing the other side of the butterfly appear in front of their eyes. On our walk home she told me how they created the picture of the butterfly and the word symmetrical dropped from her mouth. She had said it with so much conviction and confidence as though she had known and used it for years. Being a writer, hearing such a big, weighty word come out of the mouth of such a small child was a proud moment for me, and very exciting for the writer in me.

When we got home, I created the Long Word List to celebrate her using long words and to reward her for using it correctly within a sentence. It comprised a table with a space for the date, the word, and how it was used in a sentence. She decorated it and we hung it on the cupboard door beneath the stairs at her height so she could easily access it at any time. My excitement, therefore, rubbed off on her and each time she heard an interesting word and used it correctly in a sentence, it would go on the list. Consequently, she began listening out for interesting words and her vocabulary grew. As a young woman, she remembers this list fondly.

Creating this sort of thing together with a child can help them learn to love words. Of course, the child may just want to please the parent, but in the meantime they are learning a whole host of words that will help them in school work and life alike. You can use it as a spelling aid, an aide-memoire, or simply a fun educational tool. Having them decorate it or help decorate it will keep them involved in the exercise, too. Each time a page is filled, file it somewhere you can easily refer to it later, or create a new page so they can see instantly how many long words they know. These sorts of things make wonderful literary-related keepsakes.

Tip: Why not mention the Long Word List to their teacher for a confidence-building 'Show and Tell'?

Reading Together

While you might not expect a suggestion to read with your child described as a writing exercise, it is because reading further shows how storytelling is a method of understanding how powerful English language can be. Remember earlier I said that just twenty-six letters in different orders educate, inform, and entertain us? This is where it all begins.

If your child has shown any interest in reading, please encourage them further. I have a memory of my daughter bringing home *Anne of Green Gables* by LM Montgomery from primary school. It was one of my favourite books and we discussed it on the walk back. Whether the book is part of their school work or it is based on a movie they have seen, reading with them aids reading speed and word pronunciation, even allowing them to absorb regional, international, cultural, and slang words.

If they prefer to read alone, ask them questions about the story afterwards to see how much they absorbed from the story. If the book is associated with a movie they've seen, ask them questions about how it differed, if the main character looked or sounded how they imagined. Perhaps organising a mini book club or discussion session with their friends when they come over after school could be an exciting activity for some children. Also, encouraging them to watch movies adapted from books, then asking them to discuss how the mediums differed. Questions to ask young readers might be:

- Who was the main character?
- What was their mission or goal in the story?
- Did someone stand in the way of them achieving it? Who?
- Tell me how they did that. (Open-ended questions encourage fuller answers.)
- What happened afterwards?
- How did it end?
- How did the movie and book differ?

Ensure you adapt the questions for different age groups. These kind of sessions encourage critical thinking from an early age. For some readers, imagery is an important aspect of the experience. If the child can imagine the pictures in their head, it is more likely they will enjoy other books. Indeed, if there are pictures incorporated within the book, it may help the child's reading progress. Imagining the story helps your brain process the details.

Help your child read lots of different genres if you can. Discuss the main themes of each story, its characters, and their motivations. Before too long they will be drawn to specific authors and certain types of characters, especially if the book is part of a series. With experience, you will both be able to learn how writers make their characters come to life and feel like a real person.

Playing Dress Up

Getting involved with the characters and their style of clothing makes for an exciting time. Although this is in the child's section of writing exercises, you can easily adapt it for an adult and, with costs in mind, this doesn't need to be as elaborate as it might sound. The idea is that if you dress in the clothing a character would use, it can help alter your mood, environment, and atmosphere to write more in line with them. It can be exciting and in keeping with the creativity of it all to make or fumble together their clothing from anything you have at home. If you are doing this as an exercise for a group of children who enjoy writing, perhaps as part of a sleepover, you can make the whole event even more enjoyable by having them involved in making food or decorating the room as their character would have it, too.

We had a few dressing up days for school where my daughter dressed as characters from her favourite books or from history that she had learned about through books. Characters like Hermione Granger, Anne Shirley, and Boudicca to name a few. We even had several birthday parties based on books' themes. As a creative mum with a creative child, I confess I usually went a bit crazy decorating the room and making themed props and food.

These kinds of events and sessions help children's abilities at storytelling and increase their communication skills. Reading also helps us with imagery, dialogue, character, plot, expression and adaptation. They also aid expression and imagination, which are incredibly helpful when secondary school, personal statements, job interviews, and university assignments call for it.

Your local library could have summer reading activities happening during the holidays so do try to participate. Once the summer reading event is over, don't let that stop you from visiting the library frequently with your child. If you stop after the holidays, your child may associate reading with holidays, rather than for every day.

Tip: After the school holidays are over, continue to visit your library regularly with your child.

Word Games

Word games to get them interested in spelling, creative writing, storytelling, communication skills, and comfortable and confident with word use, extending their general vocabulary. Being comfortable with a wide vocabulary will, of course, help later in life, but while they are children, enjoying the excitement of words without truly understanding at that age that is what they are doing is a huge help, too.

Children working on writing exercises individually but within a group usually get very competitive. Each child will undoubtedly want to do much better than the next, so you may even feel the tension and competition within the room. If it is a timed exercise too, chances are there will be some very intense workings out. If the results are pretty good, why not have them compete for an individual and overall prize? Perhaps a book or book token? Children usually love to compete but if there is something of value for which to compete, you may well have a fantastic writing competition on your hands.

For children or teenagers who want to write something whether it is fiction, non-fiction, or poetry, there are a multitude of ways to stimulate and keep their interest, all of which can be adapted with a little imagination for respective age groups. And because everyone can learn through play, I believe each of these fun exercises can aid skills in communication, self-confidence, word and storytelling skills.

Take Away Tips from this Chapter

- Never discard a tangent.
- Be open-minded with your ideas and where they lead.
- Challenge yourself by using a timer.
- Adapt exercises for age groups and abilities.
- Curiosity feeds your imagination.
- Join your local library.

Chapter 5

Writing Fiction

While it would take a library of books to cover various aspects of creative writing fully, this chapter will touch on both its simplicities as well as its complexities. You could consider the world of fiction to be a glacier and what will be touched upon here can be thought of the upper most ice cube! That said, this ice cube is jam-packed with tools, exercises, advice, and tips taken from my own experiences. I say this because I have written several dozen books of fiction and non-fiction and published around a dozen. I have been involved with eight anthologies, ghost-written for clients, written articles, blogs, and sales copy for businesses – and still I am learning new ways to write every single day.

This is probably going to be the largest chapter in this book, so grab a pen and make notes in the margins or find the nearest highlighter pen and truly go to town. If the idea of marking this book fills you with horror, you probably won't want to turn down the page corner either, so if that is the case, have a bookmark handy because you may find yourself visiting this chapter regularly.

When most people think of creative writing, it is usually fiction upon which they focus. I suspect that could be because creativity and storytelling are so naturally joined. As this book shows, the creative writing umbrella incorporates a plethora of information from both the author and reader's point of view. Much of this chapter will be with the intention of writing for an audience, not just for yourself. So, if you are writing for the eyes of others, it is worth noting that the usual creation of a novel is not just a one-person game. There is space at the table for the reader as well. The writer writes and the reader reads. Neither can do their job without the other. It is very much a partnership. It is only that the reader does their job at a much later date.

Each time the book is read, it will be enjoyed and interpreted differently. Each reader bringing with them their own set of circumstances and influences and applying them to the story that you created from scratch. A book is more than just a medium, it is also a time capsule, and a way of stopping time all in one. It is a vehicle that envelops the attention and engages the reader until, hopefully, the book is fully consumed with nothing overlooked, skipped or glossed over. Yes, I agree. This is both a romantic and philosophical way of considering a book, but it is still worth the consideration.

Like many aspects of creative writing, fiction takes imagination, expression, and a reasonable command of language. Having a wide vocabulary, therefore, is not to be sniffed at. The more words you know and understand, the wider your resources. Read what interests you and in as many different genres as you can. Learning the different ways that context carries a piece of writing is a useful skill. The ability to tell an entertaining story, however, may take a little practise, but that's what we are all here for. It is fair to say that, even for the big names, the story takes time to get right. Editing here, rewriting there, tweaking here and major structure development there, it is rarely perfect the first time.

At this point, you may be thinking about a dozen different questions ranging from, 'I don't have an imagination' to 'what is entertaining?', 'there's so much to learn' and 'can I even do this thing?'. Firstly, you do have an imagination, but it may need some exercise to be stimulated.

It isn't just creative people who have an imagination, everyone uses theirs to solve problems, debate, predict, conjure images, enjoy feelings, think about music, practise empathy, invent, plus so much more. Our imaginations influence just about everything we do in life, from theorising dream jobs right through to thinking about what we want for dinner tonight. Just like any other body part, the imagination requires exercise to keep in good working condition. Exercise, for the imagination, is one of your biggest resources with creative writing. The more you can stimulate it, the more resourceful it will be.

To answer the 'what is entertaining?' question provokes debate because our feelings towards entertainment is subjective. What entertains you might not be what entertains me. Personal taste is one of the biggest aspects of artistic and creative projects. Some people love horror stories, while others prefer comic poetry, and some will enjoy romantic tomes in place of gritty thrillers.

You may now be wondering, if everyone likes to read such different themes, how can you possibly get it right? This is the age-old question that so many writers have asked.

Tip: Write what interests you, then you have a greater chance of writing to the end.

Choose a topic that works well for your style, not one that seems to be selling well now. In a year or two when your book is complete, the trend for that topic will be over, so focus on something that you find a joy to write. With the time and effort that goes into writing an engaging and entertaining story, having it overlooked in favour of the current big thing will be heartbreaking and demoralising.

If you are not interested in any of the characters or the plot you are writing went from exciting to dull, nothing on earth will get it finished because you are not engaged. Let us presume you intend to write a novel-sized piece of fiction that you may have been thinking about for years. The fact that story has stayed with you for so long is a good sign that you are already engaged. Check out the genre you love to read and consider why they kept your attention. Maybe that is where you ought to begin.

'Can I even do this thing?' Yes. You can. With patience and a little help, there is no reason why you cannot write the story you have always wanted to write. Removing pressure, expectation, and anything else restricting you, take a breath and focus your mind on to the page.

How Long Will it Take?

How long a story takes to write is like asking how long a piece of string is. Any kind of fiction – indeed any kind of creative writing – can take hours, weeks, even years to complete. However, you are in total control of this. There is no exact science with creative pursuits because you have to take into account the time you have available, your determination, and how much interest you have in it. It also depends on the kind of story you want to write and what you want to do with it afterwards. If you have your heart set on a piece of flash fiction that you can do in your lunch break and then file it away in your computer never to be seen again, it might take you ten minutes. Alternatively, writing a fantasy trilogy and publishing it for the world's eyes to read may take a long time.

Inspiration Gathering

At their roots, ideas come to us through our imagination being sparked by something. Open-mindedness is key to finding something to prompt your imagination because the opposite prevents anything interesting entering your mind. Depending on how you are feeling, those ideas may feel like they are falling on you from the sky or they might need a little, gentle coaxing. This is because stimulation doesn't just happen, sometimes you have to go and look for it.

There are multiple ways you can stimulate your imagination, from being out in nature to overhearing a conversation in a coffee shop. After this, your enquiring mind should take over. Being curious ought to be a part of your creative process. Seeing the world in a different way to others may be usual for you, or imagining what your dog is thinking when you pick up its lead. Joining your curiosity to your imagination, I find, is the number one best way to become inspired with an idea. My curiosity leads me to all kinds of questions, some I answer myself and others I need to research.

If exercise is your thing, wandering around the block might be enough to trigger an idea. If loud music helps, use that. If it's nature, try walking through the local woods. Whatever works for you, use it to your advantage. Perhaps it could be reading other books that gives you ideas? If so, jot down some ideas while working your way through your current read. Perhaps you enjoy the buzz of pressurised conditions, so having a deadline attached to your writing and ideas process will work. Alternatively, if that makes you go into hiding, finding other ways to become inspired may be better. Gentle activities like walking or meditating could be your thing. Why not try the writing exercises earlier on in this guide?

Tip: Ideas are not copyrighted. How you write something will be different to how someone else writes it. For more information on intellectual property and copyright, check out Chapter 10: Publishing Options.

Senses

In the world of creative writing, it is widely assumed that your senses are five (six if you count the sixth sense, and I don't discount anything when forming an idea) of the most important writing resources. It would be a huge advantage if all of yours are in good working order.

Inspiration tends to show up when our senses are employed. Listening to that piece of classical music, those lyrics, that pop melody can conjure an image that will later be used in a piece of fiction, whether that results in poetry, a short story, flash fiction, a novella, or a novel. Overhearing conversations may be a useful resource, too! One of my earliest novels, a young adult story entitled *Jenna's Dad*, was based upon overhearing a group of teenage girls nattering. Tasting something can do the same, just as smelling something. Smells, particularly, can be evocative, potentially behaving like a time machine transporting you back decades to a childhood memory. Touching, or feeling, fur, fabric, nature, skin, or indeed touching anything, can be an inspiration by helping with conjuring an idea. Your eyes are another fantastic writing resource.

We see so many things on a daily basis that much of it is seen but not registered, thus being stored away in our subconscious. It is only later that we think about it and recall seeing it, often within our dream life. Being outside in nature can yield myriad ideas from imagination. The perceived conversation between two bumble bees on the same flower head, right to the sound rustling leaves make within a vast forest, could be all it needs to write that story.

The sixth sense, as touched upon above, is not to be overlooked. We all get those feelings now and again where something is not quite right, but we cannot quite explain it. Perhaps the hairs on the back of your neck stand tall when you least expect it, perhaps when you're in the vicinity of someone you don't like or you know not to be good for you. Perhaps you experience that feeling just before something odd or bad happens. Or perhaps you can sense someone has been in your house, even when you know there is nobody there now.

These sensory-related parts of you can all be considered, perhaps, mini writing resources since a resource is a stock from which supplies are taken. After you have used these supplies once you will come to use them repeatedly, often without fully registering that you have. It will become automatic.

From here, this guide has been divided into three sections for your reading ease: Helpful Hints, Self-Care, and Techniques and Devices.

Helpful Hints

Process

In this context, that of writing, the term 'process' might be considered similar to method or system. Many experienced writers have a system or process in place so each time they begin writing their book, they know exactly what stage comes next. Knowing what comes next means they can prepare for it. Preparation can help the entire process become smoother each time.

However, processes can and do alter. They alter by writer, by project, by circumstances, and any number of other things. Having a process in place means that, on a good day, the writing will be smooth, flow well, and even be fruitful. On a bad day, however, that process may be an unattainable vision. What processes we might put in place to make writing easier for us may, at some point, become boring to us so that, eventually, words don't flow. Self-sabotage can even show up, removing any want to write at all. Should a deadline be looming on the horizon, this can make life very uncomfortable. We'll discuss whether the dreaded writer's block exists later.

Having a workable process that you use repeatedly, therefore, suggests that there is one, single, go-to, one-size-fits-all, linear method to write. However, giving this advice to new writers would be setting them up for instant failure because there is no one process. There is no singular way to write fiction, non-fiction, indeed any kind of writing. Why? Put simply, because we are all individual and from that individuality of person comes individuality of process. And, perhaps, not having a solid, rigidly built process by which to write is the way to be, especially if our brains look for ways to scupper progress.

You may have heard well-known authors say that they sit at their desk at 8am and don't move until 6pm, during which time they write non-stop, maybe taking thirty minutes for lunch. That at the end of the day they have written several thousand words, taking them forwards to the next chapter, and this process is repeated every day for six weeks. You may hear others say that they had an idea so sat at their laptop until it was developed enough to turn into a novel, which they then wrote and completed in the space of a week. Then there are those who research for six months overseas before returning home and piecing it all together. A year later the book is complete. There's the author who begins at 11am, spends time researching online as they go, and finishes by 3pm because their brain won't let them work any longer in a single day. There are those writers who begin late and work into the early hours, those who start early but finish their day by 2pm, and others who grab an hour of timed writing over lunch. So, you see, there are as many individual processes as there are writers and what fits the lifestyle or mindset of one, won't fit another at all. It's all about what works for you.

In this context process might be seen as the method you take. Although process may mean different things to different people, a process is a series of steps we take to do something, in this case, writing. Those who write regularly have a process, though that process won't necessarily remain the same for every book they write. I have discovered over time that my own process has changed with my lifestyle and needs, as well as for each individual book I've written.

For example, your process as a writer may be to create the perfect environment, ensure you have plenty of coffee, switch on your desk light, and begin writing, but your process of creating a book (or other project) may differ. Environment may be key to creating a good, workable atmosphere within which to write, but the actual process you take when writing a book is different, and could take a different stance every time.

To illustrate this further, I have written over a dozen books in both the fiction and non-fiction genres. Each novel engendered its own process, that is to say, while I may have used the process from the previous novel, it altered without me realising it, thus becoming the next book's process. Thus, each of the five novels I have written was created differently.

The first novel I wrote back in the late 1990s/early 2000s, *Dicing with Danger*, began in a linear fashion. Based upon a dream but made more logical for the story to work, I wrote a good few straightforward chapters. I approached the middle of the story where aspects of the plot were beginning to flourish. But after I hit the middle, the words stopped coming. I was stuck. I knew the ending I wanted, but I could not work out how to reach it. In fact, with this novel, I had two different endings, the one I didn't use being one that I later tried but realised it didn't make sense any longer. With potentially two different endings and a first half of a novel, I began doubting my ability again to write. Then after a break, I re-read the first half, making new notes along the way because my old notes didn't make sense now. My story had altered its path and, while I had written a sketchy plan, it was no longer useful. Then I realised, this is creative writing with the emphasis on creative. There was no need to go forwards, perhaps I could go backwards instead. To troubleshoot my way out of this issue I wrote the ending (the one than now worked) and wrote linking scenes back towards the middle so it resulted in a complete novel. If you imagine a bridge as a metaphor, I had built one end to the middle, then built the other side working towards the middle before joining the two halves. Sure, it was a jigsaw way of writing a novel, but then I don't believe there is one single right way to do it.

The next novel, *Jenna's Dad*, was written very quickly in the space of four months from prompt to end. I remember feeling incredibly rushed and tense while writing it as though if I stopped to breathe, I would forget what I wanted to include. Upon editing I added and removed chunks of text until it flowed better, albeit still pacy. As a young adult book the quick pace worked well.

The next novel, *Guardian Angel*, was different again. Instead of attaching two halves, I began in the middle and worked my way outwards like a spiral. Unless this is a natural way for you to work, I wouldn't recommend it because, looking back now, it sounds very confusing, and wound up as a novella and its sequel, rather than one single story.

My fourth novel, *Livin' and Lovin' in Texas*, was a short story before being expanded a while later. Every so often I would dip back in and out, editing as I went. I spent years doing this before it occurred to me that if I edited it any more it would not be the story I intended. Finally, I went away to a writing retreat, where I spent five very intense days developing the characters even more, then editing the whole novel. By the last night of the retreat, it was as near to finished as it would ever be. A final read through and an independent editor on board and the novel was completed.

My fifth novel had similar beginnings in that it started life as a short story some fifteen years ago. I was focusing on another book at the time but the idea wouldn't leave me, so I jotted down the notes as if I was emptying my head and able thereafter to focus on the existing book. A short time after that I developed it to around thirty thousand words and left it again. It wasn't until around 2020 after I finished university as a mature student that I wanted to get my teeth into fiction. I trawled through my laptop and found the story, discovering that I still loved it. I developed the plot and characters much further, did heaps of research and then took it all the way to over one hundred and five thousand words. After editing, it was pared back to ninety-five thousand words and became the book it is today, *Dream State*.

A lot of these processes we put in place are almost destined to fall by the wayside because the creative process varies so often, as illustrated above. We often have other circumstances going on within life, too, something to take our attention away from the focus of the project. Occasionally the process that falls away is the one that is shouting for our attention. Perhaps it cracks because we need to conduct more research, or brainstorm, or develop an idea further before the story continues? Could it be our brains find the only way we will listen to them by removing our ability to write words? If so, how cunning is that? It's very effective, if somewhat irritating.

And that's only my novels. My non-fiction books have taken their own different routes to completion. Non-fiction, like fiction, has a multitude of genres and sub-genres. Some of my non-fiction books were relatively easy to write and others much harder. While it is usually the content that makes a book easy or difficult to write, sometimes it's our mindset.

Style

Every writer has their own style, just as they have their own process or processes. Style is the way the words are written, the way the reader consumes them and reads between the lines. Style is what lets readers know who wrote the story and enables them to enjoy it.

We are usually drawn to a specific style of writing. I have found, when I coach new writers, they say they heard a big name take a specific process, which makes them feel they ought to be adhering to that process. Like this book, reading how other writers write their books is simply a guide. Their way won't necessarily be your way. My way won't be yours. The way you write is the way *you* write, and you will only find out what that is when you begin doing it regularly. Writing regularly will become a habit and from that habit a process will form. Once you've done this repeatedly, you will be able to re-read your work with an analytical eye and you will discover your writing style.

Often, publishers will publicise a book by stating something like, 'If you like x, you'll love y,' because the writer's writing style, and story, will be enough to engage readers from a different demographic, thus selling to a bigger audience. This is also an advertising strategy to help newer or lesser-known authors be seen by the readers of better-known writers.

Let's take a well-known writer. Stephen King, for example, is known for horror stories even though he has written in other genres, too. When you pick up a King book, you know what you are going to get. If a fan of his work read a paragraph of one of his books, the chances are they would know it was a King story because of the writing style and choice of words. Style is the way the book is written and becomes a kind of pattern. It will form the way you convey your point on the page. You will notice you are drawn to specific words, too. This may even happen so regularly that you may need to use alternative words because the repetition will become too uncomfortable to read.

Point of View

In this context, point of view is connected to that of your everyday world. Consider your family dynamic, your political, social, and educational point of view.

Your point of view will be different from other people's because you have different influences and circumstances within your life. All of this will play a part in finding an idea upon which to write a story. And because your point of view is yours and yours alone, it will be original. Sure, it may seem similar to other stories, but the way you write it and how you express the thoughts and feelings of your characters will be completely original because it was from you. And, just as your story will be, you are unique.

Pen Names

A pen name, a pseudonym, or a nom de plume, is a fictious name used by an author in place of their real one when publishing. Some famous literary and household names are Mark Twain (Samuel Clemens), George Eliot (Mary Ann Evans), and Lewis Carroll (Charles Lutwidge Dodgson).

Despite those famous names being known by their pseudonyms, you do not need to be a celebrity to adopt a pen name but there are myriad reasons why we might choose one. In generations gone by, some of those reasons included the need or want to hide identity, gender, social class, or marital status. Shining a light on the issues in previous generations, it won't come as a surprise that female authors were not always looked upon favourably. Most publishers were headed up by men who viewed women writers poorly, deeming that women were not real writers and feeling their male counterparts' offerings were of much more interest to readers. They wouldn't, therefore, offer a contract as the financial risk of having a female author associated with their brand was too great. Women learned that if they hid their identity by changing their name to something that sounded more male, or even gender ambiguous, the chances of publishing their book became greater.

Not all female writers chose a nom de plume because of publishing limitations though, sometimes it was more to do with how readers viewed women writing and publishing in specific genres. Gothic, horror or thriller stories, for example, were thought of to be too unladylike for a woman to write, so changing their name to something that sounded more male garnered more interest with their audience.

While social acceptances are different nowadays, the need may still arise to use a different author name. Establishing a brand with one genre, then publishing a book in a completely different genre may, for some writers, highlight the choice of using a pseudonym. Having your name associated with crime thrillers for a decade, then starting to write young adult (YA) books could confuse readers, however, even lessening the value placed on your books in the crime thriller brand, so publishing with a different name more in keeping with YA books might be a good career move. Another, slightly more extreme, example might be that the writer works in a school, perhaps a teacher, and publishes in a taboo genre like erotica. Covering their identity may be the better option, especially if they intend to continue writing more books.

Some writers prefer to choose another name under which to publish due to completely different reasons. Anonymity through choice at not ever being known as the writer, and anonymity to avoid publicity are valid reasons. Many writers like to write and publish, but intensely dislike the limelight. With the advent of social media by which to publicise our books, where people's thoughts are given freely whether invited or not, for some this can be tough to take so a different persona may be needed. Social media aside, some people just don't want anyone to make the connection between their day job and their writing life, so keeping the two completely separate by using a pen name is the perfect choice.

Letting your book find its way in the world without having an author face as a branding technique may well be the chosen method of some, although 'find its way in the world' often means that writers who use a false name will have a large team of people to promote them. Andy McNab, an obvious case to highlight, decided to keep his identity secret for many reasons, but primarily for his and his previous colleagues' safety. He is known for saying that he does not enjoy the fame that can come along with writing, so you get the impression that he, personally, would have avoided the limelight anyway. The choice has also reinforced mystery within the thriller genre and so became a good marketing tool. Who doesn't love a thriller with a mysterious writer attached?

Other big names who hide their identity have done it so they are separated from their already famous relative. Stephen King, a household name in the horror section of any book shop, library, and supermarket, who also uses the pseudonym Richard Bachman, has a son who writes too, Joe Hill. Another reason Hill chooses a different name is because his genre of writing, though similar to King's in places like the use of some aspects of symbolism (red balloons, yellow raincoats), is quite different. Had audiences known straight away that Hill was King's son, the chances are that two things may have occurred: that Hill would not have been regarded on his own merit, and readers would have dismissed his books, regarding him as 'a celebrity's son who probably got a leg up!' In this case, choosing a pseudonym was the right choice.

Keeping on the theme of genre for the reason for changing names, sometimes male writers choose it when publishing romantic or erotica stories. Readers and publishers alike seem to associate this genre with women writers in favour of their male counterparts. Some readers even prefer to read a romantic story penned by a woman rather than a man. I recently spoke to a friend who admitted they would not consider buying a romance if it was written by a man. This astounded me!

Although for a different reason, I find this fascinating as it feels like a mirror image of when women writers were not accepted for what was deemed tougher or grittier genres. Pairing male writers with thrillers and horror, and female writers with romance and women's fiction seems a little restrictive, especially as we all have our literary strengths and weaknesses.

Choosing a Pen Name

I suspect psychology has something to do with the need to choose a pen name as some pseudonyms are chosen for their strength of name, that is they seem to add weight that can reflect in the story itself, and even in sales. It is a similar thought process to creating character names when we create a writer identity for ourselves. There is also a school of thought that suggests a regal or authoritative name could have a bearing on sales. This is perhaps more important in the world of branding and advertising than for the writer themselves. Another aspect to this is choosing a monosyllabic or disyllabic name rather than a name with more syllables. Using King and Hill as examples here, both names give instant strength. Conversely, bigger, chunkier names might stick in the mind.

Writers find many ways to create a pseudonym, including finding a different way of using their given name. My own writing name for instance, is S.J. Banham rather than Sarah Banham. Even before I was married, I still used my initials over my first name. Originally this was done for the very same reasons mentioned at the start of this section, so I was not instantly gendered but now, after publishing a dozen books, I'm known by my initials and I prefer to see my writing name that way rather than my given name. I have kept the same name when writing in different genres as I published both fiction and non-fiction books. Other writers I have met use a different surname than their given name to differentiate between their day job and their books, while others have chosen a completely different name, thereby creating a new identity. I have discovered that some writers have changed their name, indeed their entire literary identity, when their older books have not sold well. I believe this to be a useful marketing tool while also being a dramatic decision to take. What of their older books though? Are they completely overlooked, or are they rewritten and republished under the new name?

Identity, therefore, has a lot to do with naming the writer in you. If your name, like mine, is a different look than the name you use each day, that separation between woman, wife, mother, daughter, cousin, etc, is different to the professional person. It is another way to consider boundaries. The name provides a distance needed to separate ourselves from our job; 'the art and the artist' you might say. I work from home, too, so it is a similar feeling to closing the office door in one room and leaving the job behind until I return the next morning. Distancing ourselves through identity or environment can be a rewarding action because without them much of life merges into one. If that happens, it can become tough to give your job your best efforts.

If creating a pseudonym is on your list of things to do, consider names that reflect the genre in which you want to publish. Ensure that nobody else has a similar publishing name, and if possible try to make sure that it is both easy to say and spell. Do keep in mind, however, that while choosing a name to publish with might be a good career move for you, when it comes to giving a talk or book signing in your local bookshop, how will your new identity deal with that? If, in time, you change your genre and create another name, what will your back list look like? Will that situation seem confusing, or won't that matter to you? It certainly is worth giving it some serious consideration.

Accountability

Accountability is a tricky word to use in this context because it is somewhat akin to something serious within your day job. Being accountable for the safety in your office or how much money staff get paid usually brings with it a punishment if it is not carried out properly. But accountability used in the context of creative writing, simply refers to you getting the job done.

Believe me, it is quite easy to say you will write a chapter, even a paragraph, and not do it. As our lives provide so many distractions – both justified and utterly unjustified – it can be ultra-easy to find something else to do but the job you intend. But, and this is the bit worth knowing, if you tell someone else that you intend to write a chapter today, that person will know this intention and with a bit of luck they will encourage you to get to that end point. If you don't write it and they ask how you are getting on, it can feel embarrassing to confess you didn't do it. Admittedly there are genuine reasons why you cannot do something you intended to do, but in the main there is nothing stopping you writing but yourself. So that is where accountability steps in. Personally, if I say I am going to do something, I will move mountains to make it happen. Being driven helps, and having a massive love affair with creative writing, but we are all different. If you are just starting out and testing the waters with your writing abilities, forming a relationship with writing is a start. As with anything else in life, small steps are best.

Plot Lead or Character Lead

I have written stories in several different genres but, generally, my go-to is romantic suspense or other sub-genres of romance. I think this might be because I really enjoy creating characters and writing relationships. While not all my characters find romance or even a friendship with other characters, relationships are often key to creating a good, engaging story. This highlights that most of my stories are character-led. This means that the character leads the story, rather than the plot. Plot-led stories often fall within genres like crime or thriller, where you find event after event progresses the story. I strongly urge new writers to try different ones. You can learn a lot from each experience.

Genre

You may have read the part of this guide where I confessed to not knowing what genre meant. I highlighted this because I find there are a lot of terms that sometimes go overlooked when we believe that by the age we are we ought to know them.

So, what exactly is a genre? What does it mean and why do we need it? At its core, genre means type, kind, or category. Category, or genre, helps both readers and writers. It is also helpful for those selling books. In the context of creative writing and publishing, genre refers to the category in which your story falls. For writers, their chosen genre will help keep their story within specific parameters. For the reader, the genre provides guidance and an expectation. For the bookseller, knowing the genre means they know where or how to place it for consumers to find. Genre plays a huge role for everyone involved in the creation, selling, and consumption of a book.

Let's delve a little deeper into genre with both writers and readers in mind. Some of the more established genres are fiction, non-fiction, poetry, with each having their own sub-genres. In the fiction category, for instance, you will find historical, romance, thriller, horror, crime, science fiction, young adult, children's, middle grade, LGBTQ+, saga, fantasy, Western, steampunk, dystopian, and so on. Length plays a part, showing up in novellas, children's fiction, YA, and some poetry. Each of these can have further sub-genres too like historical romance, sci-fi horror, and so on. Included in the non-fiction category are biography, autobiography, memoirs, creative non-fiction, essays, and journals.

The more niche your choice of story, the tighter your audience is likely to be if you are writing the book to sell. For some writers, having a niche audience means it can be tricky to find them, for others the niche readership may well run into the thousands or millions.

Some writers blend genres. This works particularly well with genres including crime, romance, young adult, science fiction, thriller, fantasy, and plentiful sub-genres of those like romantic suspense, and some genre blending like sci-fi Western for instance, or steampunk, which is science fiction within a Victorian setting and usually includes steam-powered technology. As you can see by the names, many of these genres instantly imply imagery that makes them a joy to read.

Genre blending can be confused with having sub-genres, but they are completely different techniques. Genre blending incorporates the chosen genres and presenting them in a balanced way, so each genre is given about the same amount of time within the story. Employing a sub-genre is more about using a main genre, then adding another as a secondary theme. For instance, a romance suspense story would have its foundation under romance and then have a suspenseful theme. This allows writers to be imaginative with their storytelling.

Readers and writers walk hand in hand. One cannot survive without the other. They very much form the original marriage. Therefore, it is perhaps surprising that while some writers don't consider their audience when they write, some readers don't give much thought about how their favourite author's book came into being. The writer writes and the reader reads. It is a fascinating partnership where one person leaves a message for the other person, at some time in the future, to find and consume.

Feelings and Emotions

It is worth a mention here that when it comes to choosing a specific genre in which to write your story, whether that is an organic move or you have adapted your story to fit a category, remain open-minded with your choice. You might hear some proudly proclaim they are, 'not into XYZ genre', and upon researching a little more, you might find that is because they have pre-conceived ideas about that genre. Of course, we are entitled to read or not read whatever we want and for whatever reason but mention that you've written a romance book and you can divide the room.

This specific genre is one of the most financially successful in the industry. I use this example because the romance genre, and its multiple sub-genres, is a good example of the strong separation between those who will and those who won't. When you ask writers and readers alike why they haven't considered this genre, often the response falls around the use of feelings and emotions. Some people are simply not willing to engage with the variety of emotions a romantic book will bring them, nor are some authors willing to allow themselves to feel what the character feels.

There is a third category too, those people who don't value feelings and emotions. For them, their time can be put to better use elsewhere. The problem with this thought process is that all fiction evokes some kind of emotion. That is the reason we write: to elicit emotions. We want the reader to feel what the character is feeling, or at very least, to enjoy the story because of the tension brought about by suspense.

Tip: Emotions can be shown through actions. Laughter, body language, facial expressions like smiling, cocking an eyebrow, turning up the nose, awkward coughing.

Feelings and emotions are not restricted to love and romance, just as fear and sadness are not restricted to crime or thriller stories. The drive behind those and other sensations show up in all genres, but depending on the plot and genre, will go in different directions to create the right result. Suffice to say, whatever you choose to read or write, keep your mind open to new genres because you never know what might spark your interest.

Questions, Questions, Questions

With any story, questions will be raised either directly or indirectly, and they will need to be answered. Questions usually occur at the start of an idea: What is it about? Why is it happening? What did she do? Why is he there? What are they doing? Where is it set? How did this happen? Why didn't they realise? What will happen next? Will there be a sequel?

Usually, with every answer comes a new question. This continues until the answer is found or you have dug so deep no more questions can be asked unless repetition takes hold. It pays to have a curious mind in the first place, but sometimes there is no answer, for example in mysteries. By their very nature, a mystery is mysterious and may never highlight a finite answer because one does not exist. But that need not stop you asking. There are other ways to find clues that could get you *near* to an answer without finding *the* answer itself.

Whatever the question that arises in the story, do your best to answer it or get as near to answering it, as applicable, as you can. Perhaps the answer isn't something that can be just spoken, but something that becomes clear on the quest the characters take. In this respect, perhaps the answer lies in a sequel, or a trilogy, or indeed, a series of books. There will have to be large breadcrumbs, however, because unless a story is exceptional, few readers will stand the course of a series of stories without getting answers to their questions. If they go unanswered throughout the story, that could be a big annoyance to the reader who stayed with you for the journey. Readers' patience can be limited, so reward them with answers to questions so they keep coming back to read your stories.

Research

Although the idea of researching an aspect of your fictional story might terrify you, it really need not. Some see research as boring, while others see it as exciting. It really boils down to what you need from your research. How much is the thing you're researching important to your story? You just need to know enough to convince a reader of it rather than getting involved in the intricate ins and outs of it.

Back in the early 2000s, I was writing a story that involved a character using a firearm. They had never so much as picked up a firearm before then because they had no need to. From my point of view, all I knew of firearms was what I saw on TV and in the movies which, let's face it, is usually skewed to sell the story anyway. TV shows and movies will tell you enough to convince you of their stories, but much of how these things work in reality is entirely different. I also needed to have a separate character shoot the pistol under water. I had seen countless times in movies and TV shows how a firearm discharges a bullet, even under water, but I couldn't rely on that.

Upon researching online, through library books, and asking those I knew who had experience handling them, I learned that not every firearm behaves the same way. I also discovered that some firearms will not work under water and, not only that, if you tried to there is no way the weapon will fire another shot until it has been stripped bare and dried. In my scene, there was no time to do that, nor would it have been practical anyway. Research, therefore, is time well spent to help sell your story and convince that inquisitive reader. It also taught me about different types of firearms that characters from specific professions would use.

For another story, I discovered that while human ashes can be buried beneath trees, some tree and plant species will actually die if ashes are put down. This is confusing since, nowadays, it is actively encouraged to have your remains buried under trees. The trick is to ensure that the tree needs the kind of nutrients ashes provide for it to flourish. Without researching, however, I would never have known that.

In my last novel, *Dream State*, I had to research medical and legal aspects that were vital to the story. I was fortunate enough to be able to send emails to a few writer friends who were professionals in those fields. I sent them a list of questions about the topic and how it related to my story and days later received answers. That said, that particular story was not a medical or police procedural so I still needed to add artistic license, which I mentioned in the acknowledgements.

Some stories may not require research at all while others may be filled with it. Be cautious of your sources since the internet is a well of unlimited answers yet not all are correct. Check the researched information with other corroborating sites or interview those who know first-hand what the answer is.

When conveying this information in your story, try not to paste it all inside an infodump. Paraphrasing is useful, or even better add it through dialogue or casually drip feed it through the narrative.

Do be careful when you add your findings to the story, whether you sourced it from the internet or interviewed someone, because plagiarism is taken very seriously. If you took the word of someone you interviewed, it would be a nice touch to thank them in the acknowledgements of your book should you intend to publish it, and an even nicer touch to send them a copy of the book once it is published to show your appreciation of their time and knowledge.

If adding research to non-fiction work, it matters a little less on how you incorporate your findings. If it is a memoir, you could add them in the voice of the subject. Paraphrasing works well for those non-fiction books that are not based upon people, through genres like self-help, how to, and such.

Story Ideas

If you worry that reading a story will give you a similar idea to that in the book you are reading, worry no more. It is worth a mention here that just because two writers may have the same idea it does not mean that only one writer can use it, leaving the other to suffer thoughts of plagiarism. Ideas are not copyrighted, only the body of a book can be. More on copyright later.

Narrative

I have always felt that narrative was a fancy word for storytelling. Narrative tells the story and links the dialogue. Narrative or storytelling provides story progression and helps to show character development. In non-fiction, it tells the story of the subject.

Literary Challenges

It is probable that while writing your project, you will find some literary challenges. For example, the story line in one of my novels was overly complex. Complex to the point that it took weeks to rewrite the story. If a story is too complex and illogical, this will undoubtedly put readers off and earn you a nasty online review. The idea of fiction is to provide an entertaining, possibly intriguing, piece of escapism for the reader. For my novel, then, I had to find a way to simplify it for both myself and them. If I could not find a way to untangle those threads myself, I would not be able to tell the story.

The challenge was in working out how to write and present two stories that worked individually as well as together, then interweaving them chapter by chapter making it easy for readers to absorb, with exciting and engaging characters. In the end I cut and pasted each story into a different document and worked on them separately before weaving them back into each other, thus creating the entire book. Every so often the two stories mirrored and that was my cue to go on to the next story.

I have had other, simpler literary challenges in the past, one of which is reoccurring within the writing community: where to end a chapter and where to begin the next. Usually, it is clear where to end a chapter because it is usually where the scene ends. But if there is a continuous scene that does not seem to end, how does that work? This challenge seems to fall in line with the question of 'how long is a chapter?' Many writers, new and experienced, can get caught up in the fiasco of every chapter being the same length. While this might be the go-to for some publishers, I would always advise writers write the chapter until the scene is over. If that takes twenty pages when the previous chapter was thirty or ten, so be it. Please do not pad out a chapter to be twenty pages if the scene is five pages long. The reader will notice.

Tip: Chapters should not be prescriptive lengths. Write the scene, then move on.

Other literary challenges I have dealt with are: too many characters, too many threads, and not enough plot. Chapter 9: Troubleshooting will throw some light on possible solutions.

Self-Care

It might be jarring to see a section in a creative writing guide about self-care, but please do not gloss over this part. Since the focus of this guide is about nurturing your writing development, it makes sense to include nurturing yourself, for without you there will be no creative writing.

It needs to be said that, at times, we must remind ourselves that we are not robots. We are human beings who, through all the will in the world, are trying to write a book. That does not mean that we remain at that laptop until it is finished. Sure, some writers can do that. But some of us need to take a break every couple of hours. Or maybe we need to get the laundry washed. Or take the children to school. Or make the family's dinner. Or go to our jobs. Or tend a sick relative. Or sleep.

It is really easy to engage in negative self-talk when we cannot grab some writing time. Yes, carving it out in our schedule is a good piece of advice, but sometimes the day does not grant us our wishes. Sometimes we need to practise some self-care.

Self-care looks different for all of us. Self-care can be a day off, a nap, a bath, a holiday, a cup of tea. Self-care means taking care of our own needs first. Remember the expression 'you cannot pour from an empty cup'? It makes sense.

Tip: Avoid negative self-talk as much as you can. You would not speak to a friend that way.

As a younger person, I believed self-care was an indulgence best left for others because I was not deserving. It did not even hit my radar until about fifteen years ago. Now I am older (and wiser, perhaps?) I believe self-care is an important aspect of being mentally and physically okay every day.

Before I was self-employed, after a particularly busy period, I requested a day off. The stress had been ridiculous for weeks. Upon hearing about my request, I recall my co-worker asking after my plans. I said I was going to watch clouds. I was given a strange reaction, but watching clouds was, indeed, my intention. The day off consisted of driving to a nearby country park, putting down a blanket next to a picnic table and laying down staring up at the clouds. I lay there watching clouds drift by and making animal shapes from them in my mind. It was just like meditating, restful and relaxing. It was just what my brain needed.

Tip: Watching clouds also helps with story ideas and gets you out in the fresh air, plus you can finish off with a picnic. What is not to love!

Body Clock

Interestingly, our own individual body clocks can also play a part in our writing requirements. Using ornithological metaphors, some of us are morning larks, while others might be night owls. I have heard people amusingly refer to themselves as permanently exhausted pigeons as well. The point is, whether you prefer to wake up and write before the sun rises, or like me, begin a mammoth session after your evening meal but before bedtime, it pays to know when you will get the best from yourself, and when you have available time.

Depending on your body clock, choosing to write just before you sleep may over-stimulate your mind, so choosing first thing in the morning might be better for you. If you do write upon waking, it will become one of the first things you think about. Many people have dream diaries next to their beds for this specific reason. If writing makes you sleepy, perhaps writing at night to help you sleep is best for you. While this is good as a sleeping technique, it may not be so good when you want to think deeply of plots or developing characters.

Environment

Environment can play a very significant role in your writing practices. That is not to say every writing session requires an extreme location before you can put pen to paper or finger to keyboard, but ensuring you feel comfortable in your surroundings helps get the best from your writing session. It is worth considering what would help you make your writing time go smoothly. What would help you stay in that seat and write? What can you reasonably do to ensure you will get those words down?

It is worth a mention that many writers don't need an exact environment in which to work, and many more will even turn their noses up at it as a suggestion bordering on the equivalent of 'awaiting inspiration'. However, in this context, I refer to the environment in two distinct ways: interior and exterior. The interior environment is the area immediately surrounding you. You may sit at a desk, perhaps near a window where wildlife is easily seen, or traffic is rushing by. You may have music playing in the background, or a fragrant candle burning. Perhaps writing within a coffee shop would better suit you where the background chatter becomes white noise, or a kind of music, to your ears. A library is another, obvious, writing place, pleasantly filled with bookshelves displaying books of all shapes and sizes, and storing stories and information. Our exterior environment is usually less about our choice and more about where we live, work, or spend our free time, although there is much to say about the benefits of fresh air, wherever we choose. Beaches are a particularly pleasant writing spot, especially with the sound of the water lapping at your feet. Parks, too. I have known people to sit on a blanket, picnic-style, upon a grassy bank in a park with their laptop and type away for hours. Conversely, I have known people to – myself, included – use the lunch break to dash back to the car and sit in there to write while the rain pours on the roof. Once you have an idea to focus on, your surroundings matter less than they did, but they still matter.

Talking of the weather, this plays a wildly significant part, too, as well as time of day. Don't believe anyone who tells you weather and time of day aren't useful commodities, especially to the element-sensitive writer. As with most activities in our lives, the weather can make or break them. When it comes to creative writing, or indeed many activities that fall under the creative banner, the elements can actually aid our progress. Because of the way weather makes us feel, we can use it to align with our moods. Rain can help us write something refreshing or sad, the sunshine may assist with happiness or something uplifting, and snow might fill our minds with cosy wooden lodges, ski trips, or building snowmen. A windy day may make us feel rushed or conjure images of a boat being tossed around on the waves, whereas a storm brewing may inspire an angry tale.

Writers and poets from the Classic period openly used the weather and the environment to help inspire their vocabulary and resulting works. It might amaze you how much your word choice widens when you are open to the elements and your mind is switched on to the environment.

Boundaries

Interestingly, many writers talk about how setting boundaries with their writing time can make a massive difference. Boundaries are best worked to your requirements. For me, I need my door closed or at least pulled to. I like to have classical music playing softly in the background; loud enough to hear but not so loud it distracts me.

Distraction can be a double-edged sword, giving us a moment away from what we are focusing our attention on, thus giving us a mini break, but it can also mean we might forget what we were going to write. During the thinking or writing of a lengthy piece, if someone was to enter your writing space uninvited or unannounced, that would certainly interrupt your train of thought. However, if you had been focusing for hours and getting nowhere, having a short distraction, perhaps with a hot drink and a friendly chat, may be all you needed to get your drive back in order and be motivated enough to finish the piece.

Boundaries might not be just physical ones with doors or walls that separate our writing spaces from other people sharing the house. Boundaries can exist in our schedules, too. Since working from home became normalised for many people in 2020, boundaries have often taken a different shape. As a self-employed writer, I'm often asked questions after working hours and over the weekends. Most of the time I leave those until I return to my desk on the next working day, but occasionally they need an instant response.

Breaking some boundaries, therefore, should probably be left to your own discretion, but try not to break them so often that the boundary itself simply doesn't exist any longer. Your writing time is important and time spent with friends and family is valuable, too. Allowing others to step over them ought not become a habit. Your family (and your writing time) will thank you.

Free Spirit

As mentioned previously, not everyone is made the same way. And that is a good thing for the world would not work if we were all the same. Being a free spirit means knowing yourself well enough to know this might be you. It means you may well write intuitively and instinctively. You may also be attuned to the feelings and emotions of others using empathy as a guide. You may also find yourself writing about animals, too.

Pressure

The chances are you may be trying to create your writing project in your spare time, away from work. It might be the thing you have given yourself to do to stop thinking about work all the time. This project might be the hobby you have always wanted to do, or it could be a small exercise you create as a gift for someone else. Whatever it means to you, having the project enveloped in pressure and expectation could be the make or break of it, and you.

Faced with a project that has the potential of consuming every tiny piece of spare time you have in your schedule, not to mention all the thinking time that goes into it before you even prepare to actually do it, the pressure to succeed in your creative writing project may feel overwhelming. There are those who dislike being restricted in their approach to creation, and those who, without pressure, cannot focus to even think about it, let alone do it. While some people crumble under the thought of pressure, deadlines, and expectation, others need them.

Although I am not great when it comes to pressure, I do enjoy the challenge of a deadline because they focus the mind. If you have a mind like mine that does tend to wander during writing or, indeed, during any possible moment, you may appreciate some of my preferred tips to assist focus:

- Set a timer for thirty, forty-five, or sixty minutes to complete the task.
- Don't get distracted by doing other things first. This will tire you and drain your motivation.
- Play music in the background to give the monkey in your mind something to focus on while you write.
- Ensure your boundaries are not crossed, leaving you time to focus.

Trouble Finishing?

Maybe you have a tough time finishing what you begin. There are countless reasons why including fear of it ending, getting bored halfway through, and not being engaged enough in the first place. Remember, a finished project means closure. Closure helps us move on.

Resilience

Words can uplift, empower, frighten, shock even. Consider the news headlines we read on a daily basis and think about how they make you feel. Generally angry, perhaps? Occasionally surprised? Usually depressed? Words are incredibly powerful and are weighty enough to change lives. Our language offers an immense array of word choice, which provides an exquisite palette from which to colour our stories, ranging from light-hearted words that float along the page to weightier, more powerful words that express much more than we might realise. To give you an example of this, have you ever thought how some words in news headlines hit us harder than others? While one might make us stop and think, another headline will fly past our eyes without meriting a second glance. That is the power of words.

This is the reason that we feel hurt when someone upsets us with their words while at other times their meaning does not bother us. Words can make or break us. They can empower us and they can tear us down, reducing our confidence and even shaping our lives. Did someone say something to you when you were a child that stays with you today? Perhaps they said you were not good at something and because of this, your life went in another direction?

Resilience means being able to recover quickly from difficult challenges. When someone might say something rude about your work, brushing off the nasties is needed, even though it ought not be because in an ideal situation people would choose their words with care. Because of our individual decisions of what art might be, some won't like your work no matter what you do. And that is okay. We cannot all like everything. How you deal with and respond to that rejection though is something else.

Be proud of your work while remaining open-minded for improvements.

Techniques and Devices

Opening Chapter

When you go to a book shop, are you compelled to read the blurb on the reverse and check out the first page to see if the kind of opening it offers pulls you in? Perhaps it raises instant questions by way of intriguing you enough to read on, or it might be setting the scene through description. There are a few techniques to try when opening a chapter, especially the first chapter, because if you are writing this book to sell rather than writing it for yourself, you will need an opening that hooks the reader straight away.

One thing that I am instantly reminded of though is not to expect the decided upon opener to be the one used in the finished book. Things change, stories alter, imaginations get sparked. Using that opener to start the story can be a useful holding point until the final decision is made.

Below is a selection of techniques you could try, and if they do not work this time, perhaps they will in your next project. Keep in mind that they may even serve as writing prompts.

- Open with an explosion.
- Open with a descriptive landscape, cityscape, location setting the scene.
- Open with explosive dialogue, perhaps an announcement or confession.
- Open with a controversial sentence.
- Open with a road accident just as it happens.
- Open with an instant threat from one character to another.

As you can see, there are many ways to open a chapter and some of these may appeal to you and your story. Each of these may fit your story but will require you to 'spiral' into or out of that opening line. That is, ask yourself questions about how the characters got to this point and how they intend to get themselves out of that moment.

You will find other techniques and methods for opening a story, so check each novel you have on your bookshelf. Taking the fifth option above: open with a road accident just as it occurs, this will require the explanation of how the accident came to be as well as the fallout it brings. Perhaps the accident will be the opener extending throughout the first chapter and the second chapter will continue with something like 'twenty-four hours earlier' or 'one year later', giving you the opportunity to explore the timeline surrounding it before continuing with the plot. Maybe analyse the effect it had on the characters, which, in turn, will allow for further character development.

Less explosive openings you could consider can be descriptions of the story's setting. Using the technique of many movies and TV shows, visual writers – that is those writers who use the images in their minds to help them write – might imagine an aerial view of a cityscape, then zone to a neighbourhood, then a street, then a house, then a kitchen, and finally the character around whom the story unfolds.

An example of a reasonable opening might be: 'She sat in the library holding her book.' Your reader will instantly have a plethora of questions. Which library? Where in the world? Who is she? How old is she? What book is she holding? Is the book relevant to the story? Is she waiting or reading? So, in the first line alone, you have a narrative that provides instant imagery and a lot of questions that should be answered through the narrative and dialogue.

The reader can glean a lot of information about the story from the descriptions you use in the zooming in from the cityscape to the character, so use your opening line or paragraph to utilise words wisely.

Point of View

The point of view within fiction is that of your main character and in non-fiction that of the person about whom you are writing, the subject.

Show, Don't Tell

Showing the story to the reader rather than telling them about it highlights imagery. If the reader can visualise the scene, the character, and the setting, they will get more from their reading experience. The example above highlights this.

Writing Techniques and Devices

When I first began writing, I wrote through sheer natural creativity not truly considering that different parts have different names. I did it rather like how children tell each other stories, by making up a character, then giving them a thing to do and then ending the story with a bit of drama, because that is, at its bare bones, exactly what fiction is all about. It wasn't until much later that I realised that aspects of creative writing live under umbrella terms and names, and knowing those meant I could do a lot more with my writing.

Understanding techniques and writing devices, and what falls under which category, can help you manipulate your words and meaning to get more from the story and, if you intend for someone else to read it, them too. Writing techniques provide the writer with ways to manipulate their story. Devices are those important or signification points within a plot that help it progress.

It is helpful to know the mechanics of creative writing so you can use these tools to make your stories more engaging. These were aspects I had to remind myself of over time because when you are focused within a story, you tend to be more interested in the creative enjoyment than the technical side.

Metaphor

Metaphors are one of the best techniques you can use because they are all about imagery. Metaphors are figures of speech applied to something within your story. For instance, you might have a character who has been put upon too much and the final ironic straw is having them make the tea for the boss. Describing them carrying a mug to the boss's office highlights how much of a mug they have been. Alternatively, you could twist the plot by having them set the mug down in front of the boss and, with the other hand, giving their resignation with the words beneath the note saying, 'You'll have to make your own coffee from today. Now who's the mug?'

Simile

Similes usually start with 'like' as in 'she scurried like a mouse' or 'he rushed like a mad thing'. They can bring colour to a descriptive sentence.

Prologue

While many people feel prologues are very much out of fashion, suggesting that you ought to merge the content in the first chapter or disseminate it elsewhere within the story, in my rebellious nature, I tend to feel there is still a place for it. Although that does come with a caveat. My take on this literary technique is to use them only if it benefits the story.

I would advise you decide for yourself whether or not to use one because your story may be better for it, even when fashion says otherwise.

In non-fiction, prologues can set the scene.

Epilogue

This works just like a prologue but goes at the end of the story to say what wasn't said by way of tying up any loose ends. Again, it can be argued that this content ought to be included in the last chapter or disseminated within the story. As the writer of your own story, only you can know if it is needed.

Planner or Pantster?

This is an expression, I believe, that originated from the NaNoWriMo writing challenge. This is the idea that writers are set into two categories: those who plan their stories and those who fly by the seat of their pants. Pantsters tend to write their first sentence and continue to the end, though not necessarily using one linear method. Planners plan. There is an argument for planning, it helps the structure form and keeps you on track, providing you do not deviate. You may feel less overwhelmed with a plan than if you fly from the seat of your pants.

Tip: Why not use the plan to create five lines of blurb for the back cover of your book?

Creating Characters

Creating someone to fit a role is one of the most exciting aspects of fiction. It is not just about what colour their eyes are or what they are wearing, it is about what skills they will bring to the role, how they acquired those skills, and how they behave around and engage with other characters.

Depending on the genre of your story, much will need to be considered with the character's name, the dialogue they use, the skills they have organically and those they have learned. Appearance, skillset, backstory, personality, motivations, and behaviour can all play a huge role in all stories, but particularly character-led genres.

Some author friends of mine employ quite different approaches to characters. Some put more time into creating character activities and less time into character appearance, and vice versa. One author told me they didn't know and didn't care what their main characters looked like because it was not important to the story; they let the reader decide what the character looked like instead. This further reinforces that we all have our completely different approaches to story creation.

Whichever way you choose to create them, intriguing characters with depth are paramount to any novel. In fiction, few people will want to read about a flat character without a goal, opting more for the one who flies off the page and feels like a real person. In non-fiction, memoirs for example, readers will engage with a subject who shows kindness, strength, gratitude, and forgiveness, although it does depend on who your non-fiction is about. Writing about historical characters who history records as being heartless, cold, and selfish also goes down well. The point is, whomever the book is about ought to be intriguing in some way to keep the reader's interest.

Just like in real life, when you meet someone who seems dull and has no interest in anything or who moans about everything, the chances are you won't want to befriend them. Someone who seems dynamic, exciting, and intriguing though, generally draws more interest. As a writer you want readers to be thinking about the characters even when they have finished reading the book. You want them to love the story so much that they cannot wait until you write the next one.

When I first began writing I tended to look to the celebrity world for faces to fit my characters. To a point, I still do the same, but now I take a bit of that person and a bit of another to create my character. For instance, you might like the eyes of one actor but the lips of another, the way one walks, but the accent of another. It might be a bit of a Frankenstein's Monster approach but for me it has always worked.

I learned over time that I need visuals to help my characters exist in my mind. Years ago, I would cut out pictures from magazines and tape them into a scrap book. This continued until printers were readily available and I would print out photos I had taken from the TV; then, with the advent of the internet, I downloaded pictures to paste into my laptop. The visuals create a kind of 'mood board', giving me plenty to work with. I know this system and process works for me, so when I had a story I could not easily progress because I did not have the right character's face in my head, I happened to watch a movie – completely randomly – and an actor I had not even considered was there on the screen. At that moment, I actually said aloud, 'that's Ben!'. My family gloss over things like this because it most definitely is not the first time it has happened.

You may not like the idea of taking photos and prefer to sketch the character yourself, perhaps from your imagination, to make an entirely original person. Whichever way works for you is best.

There is no one way to create a character, just like there is no one way to write a story. Behaviour, dialogue, and actions all need to be convincing to the reader because it can be easy to lose interest in the story. As a reader myself, if characters don't seem real, I easily lose interest. It is often the main character that the reader relates to, ensuring that they return for future novels because they liked the characters so much. Novels adapted to TV and movies show that the main character or cast of characters is usually the main pull.

For those of us who care what our characters look like, not necessarily so much for the reader to enjoy but for themselves to write them, read on. If the writer believes their characters are real people, your reader will because this will show in your word choice. But how do you make these things seem real?

Keep in mind that when creating characters, sometimes inanimate objects within stories become characters, too. Spaceships on TV shows often 'feel' like another character, as do cars, robots, even pets and animals.

Name Me

Identity of characters is important within a novel. Identity is not just about their name, it is also about them feeling real, having a life, thoughts, opinions and motivations and beliefs. How they treat others and behave helps them become a real person.

With the look of your character coming to life in front of your eyes, you will want to name them and you will need to for the narrative as well as other characters referring to them.

Tip: Choose a name you like, or that fits the character's role, because you will be spending a lot of time with them.

As the tip above suggests, choosing a workable name is practical. Naming your character can be a fun exercise, but one that can bring its own tricky issues. Names need to be in tune with era and genre. For instance, in a historical novel you may not want to use names like Britney, Keanu, or anything ultra-modern or unusual. Science fiction and fantasy characters may be made-up or unusual names, although that is not totally necessary. Today's writers seem to opt for short, punchy names for their characters within commercial fiction like Jack, Kate, etc, but choosing something that fits your character and genre is the best way to go. Non-gendered names like Chris, Kit, Kim etc are generally helpful should you alter the character's gender later, or are focusing on the LGBT+ genre.

Occasionally as writers we find we associate some names with people we have known before. Perhaps someone was unkind to you and their name is associated with unpleasantness, or you like a particular actor so think of their name as great. Ensure the name suits your character and blends nicely with their personality.

Once you have your main character, and perhaps your supporting characters in mind, you will want to name them. It does not matter in which order these things happen, though I tend to have a story working title, then a plot, and the characters, names and skills fall in right around the same time. The title may take a little tinkering since plots take time to evolve, manipulate and manoeuvre into the right shape so the original title may not work in the end. Once the story has developed, a title may be easier to find. Depending on your genre, a title with a double meaning can be a good idea, and some titles are the name of the main character.

Tip: Your character's name can always change if it does not feel right. Characters evolve, grow, and develop along with your story.

To help you flesh out your characters, in the research phase perhaps consider their background, what growing up was like for them, how their predecessors affected their life, what they believe in and what is important to them.

Brainstorming character development is one of the most exciting exercises you can do. Use the brainstorming exercises in Chapter 4: Creative Writing Exercises for All Ages to work out what your character should do and why they are doing it. Let's consider some ideas: perhaps they inherited a skill or curse from their parent or grandparent that works well for your fantasy novel? What skills or curse could it be? Maybe your character is a woman who will rescue her husband. Depending on the situation he is in, what skills does she have that would help her succeed in her mission? Perhaps a parent needs to find their child but an added twist that would work for science fiction might be that the parent is on one planet and the child is on another. Perhaps the child was kidnapped, and the parent needs to learn how to fly a spacecraft before they can embark on their adventure? What may have begun as a man trying to make a better life for his family in England takes a dramatic twist when he discovers they have been 'relocated' by his employer only to be used as a bargaining chip. If he doesn't do something illegal for the employer, the family becomes currency. Perhaps the genre is not action after all, but science fiction and your main character is from another planet?

Ensure you do not give your characters skills they won't use, or at least if you plan on writing a sequel or series that everything mentioned will be needed later. Your character's motivation within the story ought to be clear to you, the reader, and the other characters.

Your character's values may become important within your story too, potentially when they engage with others. For example, I once had a character Tim, a policeman, who was raised by his grandparents. His grandfather had imposed traditional values within him, and his grandmother ensured they were upheld. This showed up with how he treated women during dating. He would open doors, pay for dinner, pull out a chair before being seated, etc. This traditionally good-mannered attitude was highlighted twice, one when his partner, Dale – whose values opposed Tim's – treated women quite differently. While the two men banged horns frequently, their opposing values created a deep bond between them. The second time this was highlighted in the story was when his date, Jayne, showed her surprise at his good manners. It seemed to say something about the kind of men she had previously dated, and through subtext it highlighted societal behaviour.

Behaviour and appearance together make for a very good representation of a real person, providing your character is human. Behaviour is about making them engage with others, and touches on how they were raised.

Dialogue

I think this is another exciting area of creative writing to work on. My own interest of language began when I was quite young. Growing up in an area not known for well-spoken citizens, I was often picked up for my speech. A lot of it was picked up from school so, consequently, if I heard slang words or didn't pronounce significantly important letters like T in words like water, for instance, I would be told off. Over the years, I learned to listen out for the differences in language between myself and others, which, of course, can be a bugbear for everyone involved. However, it has made me aware of regional words and accents, international words and accents, and highlighted other aspects of speech like pacing and clarity of meaning. I share this because it all turned out to be unintended research that can be applied to creating dialogue for characters.

Dialogue in literature can alter drastically. Schooling, social classes, culture and accents can all play a role. Word meanings can alter from one side of the world to the other, and how they are pronounced.

Whichever genre you are writing in, chances are your character will be speaking to someone. If they are from a different place, is there a language barrier and is that dilemma what your story is about? Do they have an accent that makes them stand out for positive or negative reasons? Are they well spoken, poorly spoken? Does the way they speak affect the situation they are in, for example is there a class issue to develop? Perhaps your character constantly gets the word they want wrong and says another in its place? Do other characters find this irritating or endearing?

Tip: When creating dialogue, don't be afraid to read aloud the conversation.

While your characters will be talking to and engaging with each other, they also need to be understood by the reader. Poorly written or inauthentic dialogue can creep in when we are tired. To counter this, read aloud your work using, if applicable, the accents the characters have. When you come to the editing stage, carry out this exercise again. Reading the words aloud forces you to hear how the dialogue sounds rather than relying on your eyes and brain, which could be tired.

Keep in mind that we all speak differently, we do not necessarily speak the King's English either. We talk over each other within conversations through ego, conversational dominance, or excitement, and some of us do not even finish our sentences. Our friends finish them for us. All these aspects of speech and dialogue can be shown on the page but can look messy unless presented carefully.

Tip: Mess with the way your characters speak, but only if it is relevant to them or the story.

Internal Dialogue

Your character may speak to themselves within the space of their own mind. Just like we do, they may think their way through a problem, or consider what someone else looks like. Allow your character's thoughts to play out on the page as it gives them a little more depth to the reader.

Appearance

What do they look like? Do they have a classically chiselled jaw? Are they utterly stunning? Do they look like they have seen better days? In most novels nowadays, there is no need to highlight how attractive or unattractive the character is because their actions and behaviour do the job for you. Most characters do not need to be startlingly good looking or unbearably scarred to be the protagonist or antagonist, both are considered clichés anyway. Characters with flaws in both appearance and personality are much more realistic. Most readers have their own idea of who is or is not attractive to them.

Depending on your genre, let's look at how and why your main character (MC) looks like they do, and is that down to their gene pool or the job they are in? Do they wear a uniform or are they casually dressed? Does this make a difference to your story or how the rest of the characters treat them? Your character's appearance may be important to the story, or it might not. In romantic stories, you will almost always read about how the character looks, while in plot-led novels, the character's appearance is less important.

Using it as an exercise, why not interview your character to find out more about them? This will also make them feel like a real person for you.

Take a few deep breaths and close your eyes. Imagine your character sitting in front of you, a table between you. In your mind, ask them what you need to know and have them answer you. Use these findings to help flesh out their character and embellish your story. Try questions like:

- What is your role is in the story?
- Why did you choose xyz as a job?
- How do people treat you knowing you work as a xyz?
- Where are you from?
- Tell me about your life growing up?

There are countless other questions you can ask, just apply them to your story to get the answers you need.

To learn more about your characters, another exercise would be to, via your imagination, take a walking tour through their house. Walk into each room taking mental notes of their home furnishings, looking in their cupboards and drawers. Looking through their wardrobes. Learning what your imagination conjures for each character gives you an intimate idea of how they live their life, which means you can fact gather even more. When it comes to transferring this imagery and information onto the page, you can do it with confidence because you 'saw it' in the exercise. Although some workshop attendees I have coached felt like this was an invasion of the character's privacy, you have to remind yourself that they are fictional people made up entirely by your imagination. Though it is a good feeling to know these writers felt their characters were real.

If it really bothers you that you are invading privacies, why not have your MC give you permission first or even give you a guided tour themselves?

Supporting Characters

Just like in the movies where you find a supporting character enables the main one to achieve their goals, writers need them, too. You will have noticed that I make references to TV and movies when I describe aspects of storytelling. I believe this to be because my mind is filled with imagery and one way to make it make sense to others is by using these references.

Maybe your supporting character is a friend of the MC, or merely have a walk-on part. If their job is minimal and there to answer a question like, perhaps a nurse or doctor might do, you won't necessarily need to give them a name or backstory unless you intend to use them further. Having a supporting character simply show up, answer a question then never be seen again is perfectly okay.

Realistic

So, back to the question, how do you make a made-up character seem real? My first suggestion is to think about what makes you the person you are. We are all flawed in some way and so creating a flawed character would be realistic, although this largely depends on the genre in which you are writing. Creating a character who is utterly perfect – even though everyone considers perfection entirely differently – may convey as dull. Fantasy stories using superhero ideals aside.

Is that something that needs to be highlighted within your story? Is it comedic or is it sad? These idiosyncrasies help make them seem real to the reader because your character is probably just as flawed as we all are and that is what makes them feel like actual people.

Backstory

Another aspect to creating a realistic character might be to consider their backstory. Backstory is exactly what it sounds like, the story behind the person that has made them who they are. Backstories don't necessarily have to find their way onto the page, but the findings from researching them can.

For instance, let us create a character named Frank. Frank is in his fifties. When he was a teenager, he wanted to learn to play tennis. After a few lessons, he loved it and discovered he was good, but his parents couldn't afford regular lessons, so Frank had to stop. He resented his parents for their decision, believing they were selfish. Only in his later years does he wish he could have continued because he loved it so much but a strong urge to try again drives him towards taking lessons. The backstory of why he stopped is important to why he left it for most of his life before picking up a racket again. His parents' feelings towards money have also taken their toll on his life's financial decisions, and now he has his own child, he understands how money can make a difference to people's lives.

Another backstory might be that Alice, a twenty-something law student, witnessed an horrific accident when she was a child. The feelings of being powerless to help those hurt ensured that now, as an adult, she can finally do something about helping other victims who go through the trauma. Therefore, her backstory has fuelled her future decisions, albeit episodes of post-traumatic stress disorder affect her along the way. Put her into a story where she has no alternative but to help those in another, very similar accident to the one she witnessed as a child to see how she copes.

Conflict

Almost all novels have some kind of conflict within the plot. It does not have to be major and some stories have several mini conflicts throughout, but it does need to exist. Conflicts are there to give the MC a dilemma. Without this challenge, the story may fall flat.

Conflicts may be external and could indeed be a war or battle, or they might be something less harmful like a powerful character's decision stopping the residents of an apartment block being allowed to keep pets. Internal conflicts might be when someone's values are being challenged.

Symbolism

This can be a great aspect to play around with. Through using symbols within your content, you can add depth to your work. For example, youth might be shown through freshly budding flowers, direction with a compass, or age or time passing could be shown with dried flowers.

Subtext

This is about reading between the lines. It is more about what is not said in the content but relates strongly to the story. You might read it via character's dialogue to discover something important. In reality, people often talk but it isn't until you recall the conversation later than you 'heard' what they were really saying.

Theme

A theme is the subject of the writing. Whatever theme you have chosen, try to stick to it throughout the whole exercise. If you read back your work after the session is over and find you have drifted, perhaps try the session again using the newer theme. It might be that the original theme didn't have enough mileage for your session, or it could be that the newer theme was more interesting.

Themes to try are: love, coming of age, justice, survival, good versus evil, race against time, forgiveness, rags to riches, redemption, revenge and so on.

Pace and Tension

These tend to work together though also work individually. Pace is how the story moves along. Maybe it plods, maybe it spins by, but getting pace right for your genre is worth focusing on. Most stories gather momentum as the story climaxes, making the ending exciting. Creating a pace that works for your story and the genre means practising your craft. Ensure you drop interesting breadcrumbs in every now and then to keep the pace moving.

Tension can be created in a few different ways. Try creating conflict between your characters. Maybe raise the stakes higher. If your story is a thriller, having the MC walk cautiously along the long, dark corridor waiting for the jump scare to happen creates tension. In a romance, tension can occur when things are going great, then you discover that the MC is not single. Tension often happens just before the end of the chapter, allowing a cliff-hanging moment to occur.

Tip: Research how other authors pace their stories.

Blurb

For those writers who intend to publish their work, a blurb is the teasing summary you see on the back cover of books. These teasers work in two ways, firstly they impart the main points of a book, and secondly it is worded in a way that (hopefully) makes you want to buy it. It is probably the third thing that potential readers look at after the cover image and the price. If they get past the first two, your blurb might be the clincher to make the sale.

Ensure your blurb raises questions, sets the tone, and highlights the main character. Some character-led books' blurbs give more details about the MCs' dilemma, while plot-led blurbs draw the reader in with the action.

Synopsis

This is the summary of your story that you might submit to a literary agent or publisher. Synopses are anywhere from five hundred words to five thousand, depending on the submission guidelines, so do check them.

Within a synopsis, you will want to highlight the plot, the characters, their goals, and who might be getting in their way. It will need to be written with clarity and excitement. Don't give away the ending or any major spoilers. If the agent or publisher is interested, they will ask you for more.

You often hear writers telling of their hate of synopses, saying they are too difficult to write because, let's face it, how can you reduce a whole novel into five lines? Well, here is an exercise that may help this issue:

Think of a movie or novel you love. Think about what you loved about the movie or novel, who was in it, why you chose it in the first place, what it meant to you after you watched or read it. Now write it down. Reduce it to five sentences or lines. Then compare that to the official synopsis on the cover. Note what the original says in relation to what you found important. What themes did you overlook? What did you find import about the story that they did not? Now compare those findings with your own work's synopsis. Does it help?

Outline

An outline is something you would write for yourself. I have found we use similar skills for the blurb, synopsis, and outline, so keep that in mind in case you can harvest parts from one to construct the other.

As the outline is something only you will be working with, you do not need to worry about how it reads, so long as you know what it means. Include around five sentences about your plot, your MC, and what their goal is. If five sentences is too rigid, begin with ten, then reduce it to eight, then five. If you can get it to three, that would be brilliant for using this skeleton as the template for the blurb.

Tip: Reduce it to one sentence and you have an elevator pitch, too.

Editing and Proofreading

Proofreading and editing are vital parts of the whole creative writing and publishing process. If you intend to publish your work for others to buy, then I advise you to consider proofreading and editing. Editing is about making the flow of words cohesive, flow smoothly, retain a consistent tone, consistency, and ensuring the story's structure. There are several kinds of editing, which cover structure, development, line and copy. Proofreading is about checking for typos, grammar issues, and spelling consistency. Readability is important, too. If a book is not easy to read and understand, it needs help.

I have heard people say their book, whatever the topic, does not need to be proofread or edited because it is perfectly fine as it is. That may be true, however, if you have spent a huge amount of your time and energy in creating it, wouldn't you want it to be the best it can be?

Within self-editing and proofreading, there is room for a rewrite and several polishes. This may sound like going over the top with the book, but it really is not. Making your book absolutely shine is the only way to go. You will have spent a huge part of your downtime writing the story, so it makes sense and is sensible to ensure it is the best it can be at the end.

My very first novel, self-published way back in 2006, was proofread and edited by yours truly. I wrote the book, so it made sense to me that I checked the spelling and the content, too. However, in retrospect and now with years of experience, I realise it ought to have been edited by another set of eyes.

Because I was becoming over-familiar with reading this story, my brain expected what was coming next. Therefore, I may well have not bothered using my time and energy to proofread and edit for all the good it did. Picking up that book now, I can instantly see sentences that could easily have been cut, repeated words that ought not be there, homophones (words that sound the same as others like their, there, and they're) which jar the flow of reading, and filler words like 'that'. Other times I found a sentence that explained something, and the next sentence said virtually the exact same thing but with more clarity. There was no need for both, but why wouldn't I choose the sentence that had more clarity over the first? While writing, I had been totally in the zone and I did not even notice it. The excitement of finishing the book may have encouraged me to overlook typos, too.

I was tough on myself afterwards, but please don't be with yourself because it is all part of learning. This is an excellent example of why we need another pair of eyes to edit our work.

Sometimes clunky sentences find their way into your story and the only way to find them is to read your work once more. Even reading it aloud is a help, since your eyes are working less because you are relying on hearing the sound of the words instead. Hearing the words helps you work out if they are needed.

If you have raised questions within your story, ensure you have answered them. Plot holes might not show until you have finished the whole story, so make sure you have a trusted friend read it before it is published. Ensure the cover blurb fits the story, too. Plots develop and evolve so if you have shifted your story around a bit, make sure the blurb fits the finished book.

Occasionally, depending on the genre and the era in which your story is set, dialogue may be highlighted for the wrong reasons. As previously mentioned in the Dialogue section, it must fit the era, setting, and genre. Examples where it doesn't might be modern-day slang words in historical fiction and US English in UK-based stories, and vice versa. Ensure each character's dialogue is on a separate line to clarify who is speaking to whom and when. Make sure the story you have written is for the right audience.

While it might help you to have a friend read over your work, I would absolutely recommend hiring an independent editor to check it as well. If you are putting money into an editor, it gives you a sense of value added to your work. If you fully intend on publishing it for the world to read, having a professional check it over means you consider your work to be a product, which it is, and therefore you are investing in your talent. I wholeheartedly recommend this.

You can find an independent editor online. Costs don't have to be expensive, and if you have polished your book to be the best it can be, the cost will be less since there won't be as much to work on.

Rewriting

Over the years, I have written stories that worked okay. Not great, but okay. As a writer, you want your stories to read brilliantly, largely because of the amount of time and effort we put into them. You want your readers to feel the same kind of brilliance you felt when you first developed the idea.

Perhaps the story is incomplete and you cannot move further because the flow is off, or the characters feel restricted and need a bigger job to do. Perhaps it is because the story needs to be shorter or longer than you originally thought. Perhaps it isn't a novel because there is not enough of a story, and a novella is where it ought to find a home. Perhaps it is the reverse and ought to be developed into a novel because so many of the questions raised have not been answered, and the characters are too flat so need to be developed further. Perhaps the pacing is plodding and need to be fired up, or the story lacks any tension. Perhaps you just don't care about any of the characters or what happens to them – and it shows because of a lack of development. Perhaps the story has been written in the wrong tense or from the wrong character's point of view.

It may sound like a lot of work, but the only way to know for sure is if you rewrite it. It is true, often rewriting a novel can take as long as writing it did in the first place. But I tend to think that considering all the time and effort it took back then, for the book to be really good, wouldn't it be a good further investment of your time to make it perfect?

What if rewriting it sounds like a drag? Perhaps that is why the book needs to be rewritten, because it got boring halfway through and you just wanted to finish it? Check out Chapter 9: Troubleshooting to find ways of helping you through this conundrum.

Why Hire an Editor?

Hiring an independent editor will cost, but consider that cost as an investment. You want the book to look good and the flow to work well, especially with the amount of work, time and effort you will have put into it. If the book is a legacy piece, future generations will read it absorbing their roots through your efforts, so typos and rushed work will be noticed. You don't want them to judge all your efforts on one or two glaring typos rather than focusing on the content.

While nobody will hate you if a typo or two remain even after the editing process, especially if your MS has gone through several rounds of reads and edits, typos can be jarring to readers and if they write an online review it is possible they may highlight these. Don't be too disheartened if this happens. You did your best and you will be even better equipped next time you write a book.

Tip: If you independently e-publish and a typo is found, you can correct it before re-uploading.

Punctuation

I find this is a wildly overlooked aspect of proofreading and editing. Some writers really dislike the use of punctuation and others revel in it. Personally, I find comfort in using it. I believe it is a huge part of the creative writing process because it behaves as a sort of code for the reader to know when to take a mental breath when reading, pause momentarily, know when dialogue is being spoken, or know when there is a shock or surprise.

Just as with many aspects of life, trends occur within creative writing, too. Sometimes words go out of fashion and new ones enter our dictionaries. It is all part of literary evolution. It is the same with how we speak, both regionally and evolutionarily. With literature, however, occasionally the words that go out of fashion might either spring back up decades later or get lost completely. Much is debated over the use of prologues and epilogues, just as it with ellipses, semi-colons, and even commas. As mentioned previously, some believe that epilogues should be dissolved into a first chapter and others believe that they are really the final chapter and ought to be called as much. Both the semi-colon ';' and the ellipsis '...' have definitive jobs to carry out, so I believe they still have a place in our literary toolboxes and, if I am honest, I use both regularly. The semi-colon is to be used like a comma or full stop, depending on what you want from the joining sentences. The ellipsis, or ellipses to use its plural, is a really helpful tool to show time is passing. For an example, look at Chapter 9: Troubleshooting.

There are several kinds of editor including line editor, copy editor, structural editor, developmental editor and, of course, proofreader overlaps, too. Although your book may not require all those kinds of edits, it is likely it will need a couple of them.

In a nutshell, each type of editing covers:

- **Copy** editing focuses on clarity of storytelling including grammar.
- **Line** editing covers clarity of storytelling, flow, consistency of characters, their names, appearance, genders etc, locations, settings etc.
- **Structural** editing incorporates the entire story including its structure and substance. Structure is about where to place specific events so they progress the plot and move smoothly in a logical way that is easy to read. Structure is also about the aesthetics of the book. If your paragraphs are large and

without spaces between them, or have no tabs to help with those white spaces, your pages may look text heavy and some readers can be either put off or actually not be able to read the book at all.

- **Developmental** editing includes coherence, character believability, guidance with genre. Stories need to read cohesively so nothing jars the reading experience. This involves developing each character, including their backstory, drives, motivations, behaviours, etc. Keep asking why, what, how, where, when, and who of your entire story.
- **Proofreading** is the process of checking your manuscript for errors. Errors might be from spellings, grammar, and punctuation, and a proofreader may query structure and the clarity of sentences or facts.

It is possible and probable that each of these types of editing will overlap with the other but you can easily see how involved each step of editing and proofreading is, and how important each one is to your finished manuscript.

To further reinforce how needed each one is, I recommend keeping a copy of your original work and placing it next to a fully edited and proofread copy then have someone with fresh eyes look at them both. Their response will give you all the reasons you need to hire an independent editor and proofreader.

Beta Readers

Beta readers are those wonderful people who happily take on the task of reading your finished manuscript before you take the next step and publish. Beta readers wear two hats: one that reads for entertainment, and the other that highlights errors.

Over the years, I have gathered a reliable pool of readers who enjoy the various genres in which I write. The trick here is to fully edit and proofread yourself, then send it to a group of beta readers before sending it to an independent editor. The reason I do it this way around is because I will iron out a lot of the errors, the betas will give me their findings and then the editor will iron out the final few. Hopefully you will have done a pretty good job of it yourself before even sending it to beta readers.

Tip: A process suggestion could be:

- You finish the book.
- The beta reader checks the story.
- You apply their findings.
- You hire a professional editor.
- You apply those findings.
- You give it a final read.
- You choose your publishing option.

Literary CV

While you may not want to write professionally, it might be a useful idea to create a literary CV, if for nothing else than to track your progress. You might have won a writing prize, been short-listed, written multiple articles for your job, or written your child's playgroup newsletter. Whatever literary accomplishments you have, list them all.

Word Choice

Helping yourself with the words you choose will give you a considerable advantage. Consider what you want to say, and then think how it makes you feel. With fiction, feelings are as important as conveying meaning, progression of plot, descriptions of scenery, etc. For the reader to engage with the character or story, feelings are essential no matter what genre you are writing. A quick aside here is that often, by the mere mention of feelings, some may believe I am referring to love or romance, but if a character feels anxious, angry, fearful, rageful, or excited, or motivated to get something done, you can bet that the reader will be more engaged. Drivers and senses are equally as important. Imagine if, in a thriller, the main character could not smell the cordite of a freshly fired weapon when it would drive their need to escape quickly, or, in a horror story, hearing the monster approaching, or see huge, snarling teeth inside an opening jaw. Senses and feelings are, in fact, not only vital but extremely helpful to conveying excitement to the reader. If you can transfer that all onto the page, it can act as a skeleton from which a session in fleshing out the story would take hold.

When you look at a leaf quivering on the end of a branch, consider its colours, the season, how it withstands the cold and the heat. You will be using your imagination twinned with your life point of view, and physical one, too. All of that mixed up together will enable you to choose words that only you will have been able to do at that time. Only later, when perhaps you consider editing your story, will you give further thought to word choice.

Focus on writing what excites you, not what you think is wanted by the publishing world. Trying to hit that mark is a little like trying to win the lottery. What is exciting now won't be in another year. If you think back to a few years ago when shiny vampires were very much on trend, submit a shiny vampire story now and it is likely to be glossed over because that idea has been done to death (pun intended). Try not to focus on what is or has recently been fashionable and think about something else.

We writers are often asked to be original, but that is a massive journey all of its own. Of course, if you find a topic that is ultra-original, go for it, but don't dismiss other ways of looking at something usual. Just turning an idea on its head can still be original. It is just about seeing things from a different angle that is often the next newest trend, but trying to predict that and investing significant time on a novel to hit this mark can be irritatingly disappointing.

Keep in mind how long it takes and what energy goes into writing a novel, ensure you are doing it because at its heart it is something you enjoy, because you are going to have to live with it for an awfully long time. Write because you love it, not to make a quick buck, because believe me there are easier ways to make money!

On a more positive note, if you do hit the big leagues with your novel, enjoy every moment of your success because you wrote that book. Novels don't simply fall out of the sky into readers' hands. It would not have existed without you. It is a huge achievement, so be proud of yourself. Congratulations.

Take Away Tips from This Chapter

- Play to your strengths but step outside of your comfort zone.
- Learn to write on demand.

- Use visual aids, especially with locations or a character's appearance.
- Engage in your character's internal dialogue.
- Find your unique method of writing, which may alter every time.
- Celebrate achievements, both big and small.
- Create a literary CV to help track your progress.
- Edit your work.

Chapter 6

Writing Non-Fiction

Just as fiction attracts a certain audience, non-fiction does too, and while they are both quite different categories of literature, they use similar foundations. Depending on the project at hand, it is possible that the tips you have absorbed from the fiction chapter will help you in writing non-fiction.

Non-fiction has its own genres just as you might find in fiction. Choosing which category your project falls into might be your next challenge. Memoirs, life stories, biographies, and autobiographies are among some of the more popular non-fiction projects you might be drawn to. When creating an heirloom or family legacy, knowing which category your project falls into will be helpful to its creation.

Research Differences

There are some differences between researching non-fiction and fiction. Clearly, much depends on the content. Research, however, need not be a heavy job, even if there seems to be a lot to do. First and foremost, I have found that if you are already interested in the topic about which you will be writing, you already have that urge to find the answer to your own question. Writing it for another pair of eyes is just part and parcel of this organic activity.

Within non-fiction, you must note where you sourced your research, especially if you intend to sell the finished book. Take care how much of someone else's words you use as plagiarism is to be taken seriously. Ensure whatever you use is credited to the originator or it is paraphrased in such a way that it becomes your own interpretation. Ensure that you use only primary or secondary sources to back up your points, primary sources being those who witnessed the event and secondary being that which was recorded from a primary source. Putting this in layman's terms: an example would be that a primary source is information from someone who witnessed an event first hand and a secondary source would be someone else who was told the information by the person who witnessed it.

Organising Contents

Ensure photos are of good quality for them to go through the publishing process. If they are very old, blurred, or poor quality, this will show up in the final project. It is tough finding good-quality older photos, especially when they are likely to be family snaps, but if there is a good-quality photo you can use, do so. The project will be better off for it.

Memoirs

Memoirs are a collection of stories from the author's perspective. An easy way to remember is to think of it as the memories or recollections of the author. Memoirs are great fun to write if you are the author and the recollections are your own because it is a wonderful way to relive and reminisce about years gone by.

As with all writing projects, if you are not the author but working with someone to create their memoir, novel, etc, technically you become their ghost writer. Usually this is a paid role but if it is a family project that the two of you are working on together, being paid is an entirely personal choice for you both. Ensure it is discussed to avoid embarrassment later on.

Tip: Senses are important when recording memories. For instance, the fragrance of a lavender posy will help readers tune in to the atmosphere of your memoirs.

Life Story

Just as memoirs are the recollections of someone's life, the life story uses recollections but spans their entire life. If this project is about someone within your family, knowing where they sit within their family tree would be a great help with context in mind. The context adds to the era, culture, and societal and hierarchal placement.

Biography and Autobiography

Put simply a biography is a book of the life of someone else; an autobiography is when you write it about yourself. Both contain the life history of a person but may contain their personal life, their academic life, or their working life. Storytelling elements include facts rather than the emotional elements of a memoir and focus on achievements, significant life events, life problems and solutions, and noteworthy events that perhaps altered the course of the person's life.

Fictionalising Non-fiction

Interestingly, when people begin writing their recollections or stories of their lives, sometimes they can feel quite exposed and vulnerable. This is to be expected in some cases, especially if their lives have been particularly eventful. It is possible, however, to alter the type of project from non-fiction to fiction. Fictionalising a memoir or life story can help to mystify the subject, enabling them to have a little privacy and gives the author movement to embellish events.

When this type of project happens, sometimes a note is written in the front of the book stating, 'based on the life of x' or something similar. It also means the writer can be as descriptive with the narrative and dialogue as they like providing the skeleton of the life story or memoir is not lost. This can be a particularly rewarding and exciting project on which to work.

Local Interest

Not every non-fiction project has to be about a person; there is much to share about the area in which you live, particularly if it is known to have historical or other importance. Perhaps you live in an historically significant house, or near a building of historically political importance? There may even be a small, potentially overlooked aspect to your town that you feel ought to be highlighted. Clearly a project like this would require a fair amount of research depending upon what you intended to include, but including interviews with local people or information about historical residents would be an interesting aspect.

I once ghost wrote a memoir for a client that included information about a tree. It held significant historical importance within the village as well as being attributed to royal history. It had been planted as a sapling by local school children to commemorate the coronation of King George V in 1911. Now, over one hundred years later, it is a mighty oak that I drive past every day. Many see it as the tree it is, while others know its historical importance within the community.

Knowing what your book will include and its themes will help you understand how to structure it. To give yourself a healthy head start, why not check your local library, museum, or book shops for other local interest books and find a niche that has not already been covered. If you discover that all the obvious themes have already been covered, why not look at a less-obvious one? If that does not work, how about using one of the better-known themes and elaborate on it in a way that nobody else has done to make your book unique and sales-worthy. If local residents are already interested in the other books, it makes sense to find an alternative way to cover existing themes to gain and keep their interest. There is often so much material to use with a local interest project and if it becomes a book that you intend to sell, including aspects of its national or even international history, its evolution, its noteworthy people past and present, and its connections with other counties, countries, or continents would make it a fascinating read.

Don't forget that with local interest books comes local ways to promote it like social media, giving talks to interested local groups, and utilising every local opportunity like appearing on community radio as well as the bigger, national names. If your town or village has its own newspaper or information website, ask to be interviewed for it, or better yet write an advertorial whereby you are promoting the book via the advert yet talking about the contents in the editorial part. Local author book signings are also a thing, and your local library and museum will probably be very interested in hosting something similar. This is a big opportunity to form a friendly relationship with either or both with the eventual hope of them displaying your book for sale.

Information or How-To

Information or how-to books offer practical advice or guidance on something. The something might be anything from learning or honing your skills on an activity right through to personal development in all its forms.

Advice or guidance books usually show the reader how to do something by instilling a sense of fun in the topic and confidence in the reader. Sometimes these books include photographs or diagrams and other times they are text rich.

Self-Help

If you know a lot about a something that has helped you in life, this could be the area upon which to focus your project. Self-help books usually focus on the human condition and include health, spiritual, job, career, and work-related themes among others. They intend to offer advice or suggestions and are sometimes classified as personal development or self-improvement. It is highly likely that if your writing project is based on these themes and in this genre, then you are probably writing it for the eyes of others. If so, the advice in Chapter 10: Publishing Options will be helpful.

Creative Non-fiction

There is another genre under the non-fiction category that may describe the kind of project you are writing, and that is creative non-fiction. This is usually a theme that includes an abundance of facts but written using a creative narrative. Travel writing may fit into this genre, as well as nature writing, true crime, and food writing including recipe and cook books. Journals may fit into this category, too.

Articles

Articles, for instance, are non-fiction and ought to be analysed from various viewpoints rather than taking the author's version as fact. Articles are like miniature essays and are usually written to educate or sell.

Be critical in your thinking and if something stands out as being strange or odd or outrageous, research it yourself. Keep in mind that a lot of articles are usually written with an agenda. Perhaps that agenda is the author's own opinion they want to push, or the organisation the author has written for. Perhaps it is for information or entertainment only, or perhaps the point of view has a political or sales point of view. Are they persuading you to buy something or buy into something? Read, consume, and digest, but always keep in mind that whatever you read may not always be the truth, it is an interpretation of the truth.

Blogging

Blogging is an accepted form of writing nowadays. Blogs are posted online usually to inform or educate. They could be in the form of a daily diary, or by way of inviting potential customers to buy products. The origins are from a web log and over time merged into a blog. Interestingly, the word is a portmanteau, that is the joining of two individual words that create a new word.

Copywriting

Copywriting has business in mind. Sales copy is often seen in magazines and online by way of selling a product. Most adverts are a form of copywriting.

Ghost Writing

Although placed in the non-fiction chapter, ghost writing is more about the activity of writing on behalf of someone else than it is a style of writing, so can be either fiction or non-fiction. A ghost writer is paid for their skill and time, while the client is the author. Publishing houses often hire a ghost writer or team of ghost writers to complete novel series, biographies, or other works.

I compiled a list of frequently asked questions and their answers based on my own experiences with freelance ghost writing and turned it into a pamphlet-style book. You can find out more about *Ghosting!* via www.loveofbooks.co.uk.

Editing

Editing non-fiction is much the same in principle as editing fiction. Differences occur when ensuring that the content fits the brief, as in how-to or self-help-type books, that no other agenda is included than that of the topic, as in historical works, and that time frames are accurate, events and dates corroborated as well as birth, death and marriage dates are accurate in memoirs, etc.

Like fiction, editing non-fiction includes ensuring there are no missing words, typos, etc, and the flow of the content works well. Giving the reader an informative and enjoyable read is the aim.

Tip: Read the content aloud to help highlight any errors.

Once your non-fiction project is complete, you may wish to publish it for all to read. For advice on preparations for your book, and what options are open to you, check out Chapter 10: Publishing Options.

Take Away Tips from this Chapter

- Non-fiction can bring just as much pleasure to a reader as fiction.
- Research differs from non-fiction to fiction.
- Being organised with your book preparation is key to a successful project.

Chapter 7

Poetry

Poetry is one of the best-loved categories of literature. As one of the more emotional and deeply expressive mediums that falls under the literary banner, for some poetry is about articulating their deepest, darkest secrets onto the page, whether they intend to share it or not. For others, it is a vehicle for societal or worldwide change by way of political, environmental, and personal expression.

Like fiction and non-fiction, poetry has its own structures yet, just as we do within fiction and non-fiction, some ignore those structures in favour of more creative methods embracing the creativity they bring.

Poetry itself contains a kind of melody, a rhythm that draws us. This is seen and reinforced by the poem's structure, which can lift it giving it a deeper level of meaning. Admittedly, this does sound a little pretentious, but sometimes you can read a poem that somehow speaks directly to you, that is it connects in a personal way.

It is not unusual to read a poem and find it talks directly to you through its word order and structure. You might say that there is a music within language that hits all the right notes. With the employment of just the right word choice, in the right order, a poem can come to life. The beats within its structure help us consume it too, bringing that comforting heartbeat feeling you expect. With so many music-related terms to describe our reaction to poetry, it is clear to see why we think of it as a musical, moving thing, fluidly progressing its way to a pair of ears in which it will find a loving home. Because of this, it is clear how well song writing is received because of its poetic form.

But that is our reaction to it. Let us look at the other side of the poem, the writing of it and where we might find the inspiration to write it, as well as considering our word choice. Let us also look at why we might choose poetry over other forms of creative writing. There are myriad forms in which to write poetry. One of the better known is the aforementioned song writing, something most of us listen to every day without realising or remembering that its roots lie within poetry. Other forms include sonnets, haiku, free verse, ode, soliloquy, villanelle, elegy, ballad, limericks, and more.

Why Poetry?

This is a good question and will probably elicit different responses from different poets and their readers. I believe the answer is both choice and practicalities, much like when a novelist chooses that length of fiction in which to write rather than a short story or flash fiction because the size of the content just won't fit into anything else. Personal choice means we may choose the form of poetry to convey what we need to say, and how we say it, while others may feel the space, shape, and format is a better, more practical decision for expression. The short story, novella, or novel within fiction may be too large a space to deliver the words you want to write, and the outpouring of feelings, observations, or rhyming story you feel compelled to write may be better suited encapsulated within in a shorter, free verse format. Just like the structure and form of a short story cannot be extended into a novel for fear of padding just for the sake of making it fit, nor a novel's length be squeezed into flash fiction when the questions raised go unanswered due to the lack of space, the choice and number of words you want to use means poetry could be your medium. Knowing this at the start of your project can be a big help.

Big Names in Poetry

Many famous poets from times gone by like Walt Whitman, Emily Dickinson, and Edgar Allan Poe are household names. I often found that many of these poets use flowery words with confusing themes, or hyperbole that may be lost to untrained, modern-day ears. Although through the medium of television and radio, poets like Spike Milligan, Pam Ayres, and Victoria Wood, who use humour as their main driver to convey thoughts and observations, often feel more accessible since audio gives their spoken performances a life that cannot be gained from a book.

The tone, emphasis of stressed syllables, and the addition of a regional accent, plus any physical performance used, helps convey the poem's meaning as well as entertain the recipient. Whether performed through an audio or visual medium, poems shared this way can be a treat to hear as well as being educational and entertaining at the same time.

How Do You Write Poetry?

Before we delve into how to write it, I wonder if you read it? If you do, and regularly, many of these questions may already provide answers. Being drawn to specific poets means you are more likely to choose their kind of format, although you may be curious enough to try others. If you have not yet read any of the classic or modern poets' work, I urge you to peruse some. While this suggestion may lead you to feel overwhelmed at the selection in your local library, choosing just a random (or well-researched) handful will feel less intimidating. Once you have read a few from each classic or modern poet, it will become clear which method you are drawn to.

Perhaps it is the topic that attracts you to rather than the style in which the poem is displayed? Or maybe it is the meaning it conveys? However, only you will know what suits your poetic and literary tastes. It is worth noting that some poets are drawn to the music within language, that is the melody you hear and feel when reading or speaking it.

The sound and rhythm of poetry can be fluid-like in nature, and has a way of lifting our spirits, as well as deepening our thoughts and being provocative enough to force us into tackling topics like worldwide issues. While some poems move us to tears through reading just a few well-chosen, heartfelt words, others speak with a crudeness that feel as if they are meant for the dirt and grime of the everyday world yet still jolt us into thought or send us to faraway places inside our heads.

Despite its restrictions of meter, rhyme, and length, a sonnet can soar because of its design and structure. Free verse, paradoxically, has fewer restrictions, lacking consistent rhyming or metric patterns, yet while it also doesn't use any conventional musical form, it still retains a certain attraction through its fluid freedom.

Since this is primarily a book about embracing creative writing in your own way, it is possible you will learn how to write it by doing it. If you have never written poetry before, aside from a few homework assignments from your school days, I would suggest trying several different styles to see where and if your tastes are satisfied.

Like other creative writing and other artistic creations, so much of whether a poem or other piece of writing is good or bad is purely subjective. It can be written beautifully employing a range of interesting techniques, yet it didn't speak to you in any way and so, ultimately, you decide you won't revisit it again. Alternatively, you might find a graffiti-based poem carved into a tree trunk while you are out walking the dog and the words used, and the medium the poet chose, stay with you all day, perhaps even inspiring you to write something yourself (though please avoid doing that on a tree).

Many writers inspired by their senses or observations turn to the structure of poetry. Much of this depends on how you view the world and how your experience of the world is processed within your mind. Imagination, as has been mentioned before, plays a huge role in all creative writing because much of the genre relies on conveying the imagery to the reader's mind. Twin those images with the meter of consistent beats, and you may find yourself with a line of poetry that simply won't go away.

The Story Within

Some poems have a story at their core, while others seem to convey the author's meandering mind and observations, but the choice of what your poem will be about is entirely up to you. Reading other poets' works may help to inspire your choice of topic as well as guiding you in structure.

Tip: Would your story idea be better written as a poem?

It is possible that the image or idea conjured from a string of words that you may believe could be the start of a novel may find a better home within the shape of a poem.

Form

Poems employ stanzas, that is a group of typically four lines within a poem that could be considered like paragraphs within a novel. Each stanza progresses the story through a rhythm of beats that can be interpreted as a melody. The final word on specific lines may rhyme, which through its storytelling can help the reader consume and retain the poem. This meter, or rhythmic structure, is there to stress certain words, giving the poem a natural sound when read silently or spoken aloud.

Have you ever noticed how when you just cannot recall a piece of information, if you apply music or a melody to it, like a song, you remember it? This is because our brains grab that musical pattern, playing it repeatedly in our minds. This is why some children find their times tables easier to learn when they are singing them rather than reciting them. Rhythm and melody help us recall information more easily.

However, some poems do not rhyme, nor do they have a metre at all. These are called free verse poems.

Where to Find Inspiration

Our senses and feelings play big roles in our creative pursuits. Senses make us feel a particular way and so expressing these feelings helps us create. External experiences create internal ideas. You may hear a song writer say they wrote their song because they experienced heartbreak, or a novelist confess their inspiration was through people-watching in a café. Maybe an artist painted their interpretation of a forest not in the greens and browns you might expect, but in reds and blues because those colours represented what he or she felt. Poets generally work on the same principle: interpretation. It is a way to process our thoughts and feelings.

Perhaps we see, smell, or experience something that stays with us, or we might hear someone's words that remain with us. Maybe the words mean something personal to us at that moment or else force us to reminisce about an experience from years gone by. Those words that then rumble around in your subconscious for a while before returning to your conscious mind and, through interpretation, a line of poetry falls out of your head, metaphorically speaking, of course.

It is also possible that a poem can come to you when you are not looking for one. That is, when you are not 'seeking inspiration', somehow the poem still finds you. In this case, jot down the words or describe the images to see how you can mould them into the right format for their meaning.

What to Include

This is tricky to answer since what excites one writer won't necessarily excite another. Maybe you are in the mood for something serious, or light-hearted or comedic. It might also be an outpouring of emotion, anger, or grief. If you find that writing a poem incorporates the two moods, perhaps dark comedy is where your story sits? Although, the manifestation of your poem might not be as linear a process as that. However, if you are just starting out with poetry, try not to be too restrictive; allow yourself space to develop. Encourage yourself to write poetry for the fun of it before you set expectations. It is often best to 'empty your head' and see what comes out. You can always shape your findings into a specific structure or form later.

If you find yourself writing a story within the poem, the structure of the stanzas can enable tension to build through your storytelling and allow you to tie it all up nicely with a final climactic stanza.

Environment

As mentioned in Chapter 5: Writing Fiction, creating an environment in which to write can be a good idea to help express yourself. If loud noises or a cold or hot temperature is just not your thing, work on your project indoors. If the restrictive nature of your room is not working for you, try a coffee shop where the cacophony of voices produces a white noise that becomes natural background music. Perhaps take a notebook to a nearby park and, while you watch the swans paddle by in the pond, something interesting will form inside your mind? The trick is to not fill your mind with expectation unless that is your preference, and you work better under pressure.

Tip: Allow the words to simply flow, like breath. Breathe in, close your eyes, and exhale.

Word Choice

While word use and meaning is a hugely important part of any creative writing project, for without them there is no writing, within poetry meaning seems more vital. Poetry does not usually have a very big space to convey meaning so it has to work harder to be successful. Much like flash fiction, that is stories of one hundred words or fewer, poetry relies on powerful words that carry huge weight. When you have such a small space to get across the emotions, meaning, and intention, the word choice needs to be precise and kept succinct.

Through the mixture that is our senses, feelings, and interpretation, you are drawn to meaning, and perhaps even the shape of specific words that explain perfectly how you feel or what you want to say. Some have double or deeper meanings, so using the right ones to interpret can be a tricky process at first. Keep trying, though. Everything takes a little practise, nurturing, and patience to develop. Some words seem instantly poetic and are straight away at home within a poem, while others need to be chipped away to fit the space, like a sculpture, and suddenly your poem takes shape.

Rhythm

Rhythm is the beat sound that helps form both the story and the melody. The stressed syllables help create the rhythm. It is like a pattern and finds a natural home within poetry. It's the boom-boom, boom-boom heartbeat sound, feeling, sensation that we all learn before we are even born. Used well, it is possible the reader won't even realise there is a rhythm there, especially if they are utterly focused upon the words and meaning, because the rhythm forms a natural part of the experience.

For beginners to creative writing and poetry, think about the kind of music you generally enjoy. Is there a specific beat you are usually drawn to? Perhaps it is more boom, boom, boom? Once you know the kind of poem you are writing and know the rhythm you want, you can experiment with some. For instance, perhaps the first two lines in your poem are rhyming, then the third line does not, but the fourth joins the first two. To add some interest, perhaps the third line in the second stanza rhymes with the third line in the first, thus creating a pattern all of its own.

Life Cake

Take a piece of you, (5 beats)
And take a piece of me, (6 beats)
Add a cup of life, (5 beats)
And mix it lovingly. (6 beats)

Sprinkle in some happiness, (7 beats)
Throw in some highs and lows, (6 beats)
Bake it for a lifetime, (6 beats)
And watch it as it grows. (6 beats)

Capture all the friendships, (6 beats)
Stir in all the fun, (5 beats)
Ice it with fond mem'ries, (6 beats)
Then savour, everyone! (6 beats)
©2018 S.J. Banham

Tip: Use punctuation to benefit your poem's structure. An apostrophe replaces the missing syllable above, emphasising the rhythm and beats throughout this story through verse.

Techniques

As with other genres of creative writing, poetry uses a set of techniques that help to write, manipulate, and polish your completed works. Poetry employs rhythm, beats, and melody to create the body but, inside the poem, there are techniques that emphasise and reinforce its meaning. Carry out your own research on the techniques that appeal most to you, and how they can benefit your style of poetry.

Basic Poetry Techniques

- Personification lets you give inanimate objects human feelings and actions. For instance, water *runs* down a rock face, a cake *sits* on a plate, a broom *stands* against a wall.
- Assonance is repetitive technique shown with the sound of similar-sounding syllables close by like 'Kate baked cakes'. Each work has the 'ay' sound. Another example is 'hail, bale, sail'. Even though the spelling is different, the sound is the same.
- Alliteration utilises repetition of the initial letter like 'Betty's beautifully baked buns'.

While there are many techniques to try, why not look at compiling your own list of weighty, powerful words with different syllables to gather some pretty fluid, yet meaningful words? Why not 'collect' words that you enjoy the meaning, the look, and the shape of, then separate them into separate columns of one, two, and three (or more) syllables. Afterwards, when you come to that time when you just cannot find the right word that conveys what you want it to, you can go to your list of words and choose the right one.

Talking of bare bones, some poems are constructed from the fewest words possible but carry the heaviest or sweetest of topics. If they create the weightiest, most powerful images, it is often these poems that become giants, making us feel they can change the world for the better.

Tip: Some poems work better spoken aloud.

Poems are often made better by reading them aloud. The melody provides a better experience this way. Rhyming brings its own fluid melody that enables the listener to predict and expect specific words. For comic value, you can leave out the word completely, leaving them to hear it in their heads anyway. Alternatively use a non-rhyming word in its place that throws the melody and can add humour. Obviously much of this is down to the reader's delivery and performance.

Lastly, expect some frustration when writing poetry. Like most forms of creative writing, there will be times when whatever you want to achieve just won't work despite putting in place every little thing you can think of. In cases like this, trace your steps backwards to see if the issue can be solved with logic, or if you simply need a break from it. Once you return, chances are you will see your poem is a lot better than you first imagined.

Poetry Exercises

- Write a poem of your choice and length using alliteration. Every first letter of every word must be the same and the poem must make sense.
- Write a poem of your choice and length using assonance. Every word must use the same sound and the poem must make sense.
- Write a poem of your choice using every letter of the alphabet as the first initial. It must make sense.

Tip: For extra tension, add a timer!

Or try a different kind of exercise:

- Keeping the senses activated, describe five smells/aromas in the room and use as many words that define them as you can.

- Describe five sounds you can hear from your position in the space you occupy.
- Describe five objects you can see in the space you occupy.
- Describe five things you can touch from your position. For added excitement, and if you want to make it a game with friends, add a timer. Read out your findings afterwards.
- Create a selection of your own poetry-related exercises to use in the future. Use them to give your brain a quick but intense workout before you write for real, or just use them for fun. The choice is yours.

Poetry Groups

Just like I suggested for writers of fiction and non-fiction, as a poet you will want to find your people. Like-mindedness is a huge help to individual creativity and development. It is likely there are many people in your area, in online, who would enjoy the sense of community a group offers. If you are the person who delights in bringing your kin together, why not create your own poetry group? If you prefer to let someone else organise community groups, do your research to see the kinds available. Don't be shy in asserting your needs. If you don't think a group is for you, try elsewhere online or in the next town if you want to attend in person.

Some groups may indulge in spoken word events, and others may simply revolve around regular meet-ups of writing poetry then reading it out so other members offer feedback. Some may even encourage brainstorming because the gathering of ideas within a group can be refreshing and helpful, especially if you find you have run out of hooks upon which to base your poem.

Remember that creating your own in-person group that has an ethos or set of ground rules may be useful from the start. That way everyone will know what to expect and what is expected from them. Check out the Writing Fiction chapter for further advice on writing groups that includes suggestions for online groups, in-person ones, decisions to make, logistics, venues to consider, fees, and gathering volunteers to help create a regular community meeting.

As with regular writing groups, after groups have settled and a core membership is clear, you may find the collective needs going in a different direction to that stated originally. If you are the lead member, organiser, or host, do ensure the original ethos is adhered to. Alternatively, if the new needs are better and the group has evolved, rewrite the group aims to show this so new members know where they stand. Any confusion can gather problems quickly.

Groups that work well together are a blessing in which to participate, but sometimes members come and go so a different dynamic is apparent and character clashes occur. If you are the lead and find you are dragging your feet getting there or find yourself sighing deeply before you arrive, perhaps things are not swimming along so smoothly.

I have often found if you open a line of discussion for all to offer their thoughts, you might end up with even more problems to solve, especially if members show up with problems but no solutions. That said, it is not a therapy group, and you are not there to solve everyone's personal issues. If members have potential solutions to the problems that arise, ensure they feel comfortable airing them so everyone benefits.

While I have always run my groups fairly, it is okay if not everyone agrees with the solution. We cannot please everyone all the time, we can only do our best for the majority. It might be that the member with the problem is actually at a group they do not like anyway, and keep in mind some people simply enjoy highlighting problems and ruffling feathers.

If you are the lead and you cannot make the session through something unavoidable, ensure you have a 'second-in-command' who you trust to make important decisions in your absence. If you hold the meetings in a local library and the staff are also members or are managing the group, take any problems to them as they will have a structure in place for situations like this.

With any community group it might be useful to have a social media platform, like WhatsApp, too. This lends itself to provide a way to discuss things quickly or ask and answer questions rather than emailing, phoning, or having members show up on your doorstep when you least expect it.

Take Away Tips from this Chapter

- Read poetry in all its forms, both classic and current poets. You may learn something new you can apply to your own work.
- Experiment to find a style or styles that suit your poetry.
- Be patient – nothing worth doing is instant.

Chapter 8

Legacy Writing

Have you ever considered that you may have a true story to tell? Perhaps a member of your family has led an interesting or unconventional life? How someone spent – or is spending – their life, is a great attention grabber for a book. People love to read about how other members of their family lived and worked.

The stories of everyday people ought not be overlooked. Maybe you heard family members reminiscing and feel their story ought to be written down rather than allowed to be distorted over time, or worse, forgotten. This is one time when we realise if we don't record the memories, they could be lost forever. That thought alone feels frightening, so if we can be proactive about that, then so much the better.

Writing the history can be fascinating because we can learn so much. Sometimes these books are created simply to hand down the generations and other times they are created by way of a gift to another member of the family. For instance, if your grandparents are approaching a milestone wedding anniversary, why not put together a book of their lives converging at their wedding day or starting from their wedding onwards to present day? The memories remembered each time they open the book would be worth the effort of creating it.

It isn't just about nostalgia either. We can learn a lot from family history. Aside from discovering the everyday lives of our ancestors, we can also gather information about culture, society, historical events, the politics of the time, and so much more. Cars, transport, and fashions are usually interesting focal points within family-based stories, especially if there are photographs involved to back it up. Architecture plays a part, too. How many family photographs have you seen with people posing for the photographer outside a church, a house, on a housing estate, on holiday, abroad, a holiday camp, etc? Everything within the picture will give us a good idea of what was considered normal life at the time. Small observations from photos help us see how things have changed within society, like smoking in public buildings or children sitting on the roadside with a straw inside a glass bottle of pop while their parents enjoyed a drink inside the pub.

As previously mentioned, however, not every story would be interesting to a wider audience, even if it sounds amazing to you. The advice here is to think hard before expecting the story will be published for the world to read. I have heard too many people say they think their story is the best thing ever and that they believe a publisher will instantly pay them millions of pounds for it, or that it would be an instant bestseller, or even that a publisher would be lucky to have their story at all. There is, of course, nothing stopping you from submitting your story to an agent or publisher for a traditional publishing contract, but please be warned you may be in for some disappointment as not every story has bestseller material attached to it.

On a more positive note, this does not stop you from creating your own book containing the family stories. Creating a one-off or a few copies of a book purely for family and close friends is an entirely possible activity that, I believe, ought to be done by more people.

Writing for the love of it and recording memories for future generations to read, learn, and understand about their relatives is one of the most rewarding projects you can do. Whether one copy or ten exists, it does not matter. The fact that it exists at all is the most important thing. It is now an heirloom and can be considered a legacy because of what it contains.

What to Include?

The idea sounds amazing but what should you include? Have you ever been to a family event, perhaps a wedding, birthday party or funeral, and found you were discussing the extraordinary things someone got up to when they were younger? Aunt Edna may well have been one of the volunteers in the London 2012 Olympics. What did she do each day within those two weeks? Who did she meet? Did she have photos taken with any gold medal winners? Did they keep in touch with her? Maybe Uncle Bill's ten-mile cycle to school every day put him in good stead to compete in county cycle races, which he won two years' running? Maybe he still has the trophy to show for it? Does he treasure it as it sits on the mantelpiece, or is it in a box of junk in the shed, unpolished and forgotten? Maybe your mother was the dinner lady at a school attended by someone famous, or your father's army career took him to overseas locations that make you want to visit them now? Almost anyone's life can be seen as interesting, it is simply all about how you view it and what you want to highlight.

Including things like daily life, social and family pressures, jobs, events, etc are sure to be a hit. Other projects may include passing along old skills to future generations like woodworking, recipes (an exciting idea!), dressmaking and niche subjects like letter writing, why they began, who their pen pals were, where they were located, and including copies of the letters. Future generations may not have the opportunity to work with their hands as past generations did, so recording these skills and highlighting why they were important to learn will be an extra special legacy read.

Taking on a project like a life story, biography or a memoir need not be overwhelming. Once you know the difference between each, it will make life easier about what to include. Keeping each step organised will assist the smooth flow of your process. Check out Chapter 6: Writing Non-Fiction for more details.

What are the expectations? That is, do you intend to print copies of a finished book for all the family, or will it be a one-off, home-decorated collection of memories? Whichever is the type of project you intend to write or be part of, it would be worth having a plan, at very least a vague one, of what to include. At the roots of each story is a person, so knowing something about that person, when they lived, how they lived, what their job was, a bit about their family, their drives, their hopes and dreams would be of great importance to the content.

If there exists a selection of photos to both back up these experiences and provide a pictorial reader experience, they can be included. While text-heavy books may be loved by many, it helps some readers to have that text broken up with pictures, and of course it is a great feeling to see photographs of your relatives in different times. A veritable family treasure!

The next step would be what, exactly, is the information you would be recording. You may need to interview the person or, if that is not possible, someone else who knows about these stories. As stories are told over the years, some become embellished, skewed and twisted, and even become different stories altogether. Assuming this book is purely for family and friends' consumption, and not for selling, if stories become embellished it does not matter too much.

It would be a courtesy to let everyone involved know the book is to be written. As soon as that information is out, I suspect most people would instantly want to know what was going to be included. On the plus side, it could mean you would have more stories properly corroborated and, indeed, more stories altogether. Be sensible with what you hope to include and consider peoples' feelings. Avoid writing anything nasty about others and especially don't name them if you are. At best this is bad manners and at worst it can lead to legal issues.

If the book is to be published for a worldwide audience, undoubtedly you will have an agent or publisher on board, and an editor, who can guide you with what is legally okay to include and what may be considered problematic. For instance, if there was a negative incident and people are named, it is reasonable to conclude that recording this for all to see is not the best way forward.

Entering into a project whereby you may be interviewing members of the family can highlight some tricky logistics. From experience, I know that it can be difficult to get them to agree to it in the first place, and even if they do, arranging frequent interviews is not always the easiest thing. In most cases, the term 'interview' does sound quite formal, so perhaps consider them 'chats' instead. This in itself may help things feel more relaxed and when people are feeling relaxed, it is usually quite difficult to get them to stop telling you about their memories.

At this point, it is worth using a voice recorder as well as jotting down notes because later on when it comes to writing the book, you will need to refer back to names, places, and events. People generally get quite excited when they reminisce, so will talk for hours. Knowing how to edit down the telling and retelling of the same event will be helpful to you or else you will be overwhelmed with the same event from seventeen different angles and have enough material to fill the book by itself.

If this is the kind of thing that might occur, draw a timeline with dates and times that may help the interviewee recall what went first. Much confusion can occur if people throw their recollections into the air, hoping they fall exactly where they are expected. If several relatives are attending at the same time, have them talk at different times so as not to confuse matters further.

At the end of the recollection of an event or incident, it would be helpful to read your notes to the subject to ensure you have left nothing out. Chances are they will add to it again, so do make more notes if you don't already have that snippet of information. Hearing the subject reminisce and tell the same story four times will help you capture their distinct voice. Capturing their voice is a beautiful thing to include as they will have specific words they will use through habit, perhaps regional and slang words, too. All this goes into the mix of creating someone's distinctive voice.

It is always a wonderful, if somewhat poignant, addition to the project if you did record their voice or film them during chats, and certainly something to keep for when the inevitable happens. Family members are certain to treasure it all.

If you are writing a book about a deceased person, you will have to rely on the stories from other family members, ensuring that their recollections tally. If corroborating certain events proves too tricky, perhaps come back to that event later on in your process, thus allowing yourself to return with fresh eyes. If no relatives are old enough to remember, you will have to gather as much information as you can through photographs, records' offices, possibly even the library or a museum depending on what the book is covering. Don't forget to try online resources such as www.ancestry.com. Another book that would prove hugely helpful here is *Writing Your Family History: A Guide for Family Historians* by Gill Blanchard.

Legacy projects are not always enveloped in such pressurised situations. However, time may still be of the essence. If this is the case, create a spreadsheet with the deadline and plan to write (and interview) x amount per day to reach the goal.

Sometimes creating a legacy project is less of a challenge than you might think, and people write their own life stories, memoirs, or other book without the need for help.

Through looking for something else, I recently found the memoirs of two relatives. One was by my grandmother's brother, Joseph, and the other was by his wife, Edith. It appears these two people were a very literary couple. Perhaps that is where my love of writing comes from? Joseph wrote a hardback book, barely bigger than a man's palm, on the topic of engineering. Within this book there are illustrations. In Edith's book, her memoirs, however, was a plethora of social history.

Edith's book, more of a pamphlet than the hardback book by her husband, was stapled through the middle and twice the size of the hardback. The book was printed in 1977. Within the first page, she had written a personal message to my grandmother – her sister-in-law. This makes it even more or a family treasure because of the example of her handwriting. Further in, she talks about her family, the First and Second World Wars, people who lived close by, social thoughts, her own thoughts, general life, daily food, and some rhymes that were commonplace at the time. Some of these themes could be a good starting block for other projects.

Further into the book, which covers life before and during both world wars, you get a taste of how social classes were considered and how, while her class was very much the bottom of the tree, she was very intelligent. Leaving school at fourteen had a traumatic effect on her because she thirsted for knowledge and knew that life had a plan for the likes of a young girl even if she was going to fight that plan.

She lived in service after having lots of different jobs over a period of three years, mentioning that some of those jobs were intended to be short-lived, and that others did not suit her at all. As I read, I noticed she didn't sound like the kind of person who would take any cheek either. She was strong-minded and added a fair chunk of cynicism, sarcasm, and humour to the book. This added a human dimension. Rather than recording fact after fact, it is more about feelings, intentions, and daily life. While the spelling and punctuation is occasionally jarring, it is quite clear this woman had a brain and would use it no matter who told her not to. She included photographs, pictures of ration books and certificates, which gives a good idea of what you could include in yours.

This is absolutely the kind of thing that I love to know about previous generations of my family. It is a treasure trove of knowledge. I appreciate that other writers within my family came before me. It may say something of my own feelings of getting stories and non-fiction completed before my time is over. Leaving a legacy is one thing but knowingly and deliberately creating it is another. Knowing where we came from gives us a good bearing to know where we are going. If you have a willing family member to interview, the resulting book would be an amazing find for future generations to read.

I realise the two books are entirely different through their printing and their content, and it is particularly interesting to see that Joseph's book is bound professionally. It makes me wonder if this decision had any bearing on whose was considered to be of more importance? Joseph's potentially for men to consume and Edith's for other women. Despite these differences, both are still excellent social records, family history treasures, and heirlooms, proving that 'ordinary' is more than interesting, it is extraordinary.

Tip: Consider drawing a family tree to help you work out who originated from where.

Organisation

Being organised is key to any writing project, but for this kind, it is even more important, especially if you are borrowing original material such as photographs to scan. I once ghost wrote a memoir and was offered thirteen ring binders completely filled with photographs in plastic wallets. All the photos were intended to be included in the book, until I explained that it would require several books purely of photographs and no text. A pictorial history is one thing, but that was not what I was hired to do. Once we had whittled down the photos together – which took an entire session, removing the duplicates and similar photos from the same event, as well as people who were not connected with the events to be included, we finally got somewhere. It is a tough choice to make, but if the book is to be a retelling of their life or recollections, having more than is needed will created a huge amount of unnecessary work. While they would have been wonderful to look at, it would have resulted in a very expensive photo album.

Gathering information can take more time than the writing. Be patient and careful with original documents. Depending on the age, you may not be able to get another copy.

Tip: Remind yourself of the original brief as it is easy to get over-involved.

Anthology

If your project is less of a memoir of one person, and more of a collection of stories from the same group or family from each of their perspectives, organisation is still key and, in fact, may well be more so.

If you are the designated organiser or writer of the project, I advise you to have one or two people roped in to assist. For example, let us say you have a community group with recollections of when the King visited the village, you would want a couple of volunteers to help you gather experiences and collate them in case they are in digital, voice, or written format.

Once collated into one document, probably digital via scanning, it would be a good idea to have at least two volunteers willing to proofread and edit, should any edits be required. If the resulting book is to be printed and sold, perhaps for charity, do ensure that everyone has signed an agreement to this effect before the book is printed. You don't want anybody getting upset that they didn't want their words in print, especially after all that effort has been made.

Collection

Similar to an anthology, a collection of stories, recollections, etc, is usually from the same author. A writer of short stories, for instance, would gather a set amount and publish them under a collection. The collection may be of a single or multiple themes but is always from a single author.

Sessions and Equipment

While we all have our own ways to proceed, I advise having a routine that works with the subject's schedule if regular chats will be taking place. Ensure you agree on an amount of time for each session. If they are elderly, they may get tired easily and their memories could get easily jumbled. Perhaps an hour or two at first, and later when things start hotting up, maybe you can spend an afternoon together digging deeper into specific events.

Doing this over a cup of coffee is usually the best way since the subject will be relaxed and open up. Use a voice recorder or a mobile phone and make notes. This way you can tally the two together when you need to refer to either, especially when marrying specific events and word use.

Interview Techniques

I have found ways to proceed with questions, although you may well find others that work well for you and your interviewee. Once settled, you can then begin with a selection of obvious questions like, 'Tell me about the house you grew up in', or 'Let's talk about your parents'. Don't be too worried at this stage if you are not sure what kind of questions to ask, you may find that as they reminisce questions make themselves known organically.

Rather than interrupt the subject's train of thought, jot them down to ask when a natural break occurs. Alternatively, have a set amount of questions that are open-ended that force them to speak. If you ask a yes or no question, it won't give you as much scope as open-ended ones. Try something like, 'Tell me about your first job', and just try to keep up with the onslaught of memories!

When it comes to reminiscing, get them to use their senses and emotions. Ask them to think about how they felt, what they saw, heard, said, even smelled or tasted, or how something felt when they touched it. They may remember how their favourite dress felt to the touch and while wearing it, or how high their shoes were and how they staggered when they walked or how many blisters were on their heels when they took them off. Perhaps they remember the fresh scent of cut grass when their father mowed the lawn, or the scent of the brand new car they had when the rest of the neighbourhood didn't have one yet, and see how that memory inspires others. Getting them to re-experience the event will add flavour to the final piece and senses, especially fragrances, are fantastic stimulants that unlock memories as if they were keys.

Try to keep their voice, that is their style of speaking, when you transfer their words to the book. It makes a massive difference to the reader as they will 'hear' the subject in the words as if they are speaking directly to them. Bear in mind that whatever software you use to write the resulting book may not like slang or regional words, or those with poor grammar, and may highlight them all in red. It is your choice, or that of the subject, whether or not the King's English is the way forward on that project. Personally, I really enjoy hearing the way people really speak coming through when I read biographies.

Not everyone speaks perfect English and nor should they. Regional words and slang often convey the point they are making a lot quicker and easier than trying to transfer their words back into the kind of English you would expect from newsreaders. If this project is for the family, reading a few local words within the content would reinforce the subject's personality and help future generations understand them a whole lot more. It makes the project very personal, too.

Later down the line, when you are ready to collate the entire project into a book format, scan photos, handwritten letters, and official documents into your computer to ensure crisp, clear images. Read Chapter 10: Publishing Options for ideas on how to create one or more printed copies of this book for your family.

Tip: The better the image, the better the outcome.

Gathering the handwritten letters, certificates, and photographs of a subject, then creating a front, back and spine or even simply holding it together with ribbon makes this a completely original piece of craft. Making this highly original project ensures there is only one copy, and thus it becomes even more precious and valuable to the family.

A word to the wise: please consider using copies of legal documents like birth certificates rather than the originals. Once they are attached to the hand-made book, removing them can ruin the entire project or deface the documents.

Wrap it Up

There are books available that offer step-by-step guidance on creating a one-off physical book like *Bookbinding and How to Bring*

Old Books Back to Life by Aimee Spillman. This retains the hand-made craft element, which is beautiful yet keeps things looking neat and tidy, and is also practical for people to handle.

How about punching holes in handwritten pages and fastening them with pieces of string? That may not be the most secure method but for a special gift, boxed and wrapped in tissue paper, it surely would be a sentimental gift. Similarly, consider typing the content but printing it on different pastel or bold-coloured paper before adding the holes and string? Perhaps by adding lace and silk flowers to the front cover of a handwritten memoir it can become a wedding or anniversary gift?

Just as a novel has plentiful ways to progress, develop, and evolve, a little imagination and some craft supplies can create a beautiful one-off heirloom for family members to pass down the generations. A delightful legacy piece, for everyone to treasure.

Take Away Tips from this Chapter

- Keep things as simple as possible.
- Form a plan.
- Stay organised.
- Gather as much assistance as you can.
- Consider creating a one-off individual book.
- Ensure the final outcome fits the brief.

Chapter 9

Troubleshooting

The mind of a writer is a fertile environment. We all want to get on with the work and throw ourselves wholeheartedly into the project. The sooner it is complete, the sooner we can move right along to the next piece of writing because our minds are usually filled with a million other ideas to flesh out. However, there are also times when our minds are anything but productive, or they are productive in giving us problems.

Sometimes the problem is small and other times it's a lot bigger. It could be writing related or writer related. It may niggle or stop progress altogether. The one thing that has always helped is analysis. If you take a step back and really look at the issue from another angle you may be able to see how to solve it.

There are ways to prevent, avoid, or resolve problematic activities that may alleviate the situation in which you find yourself. Another read of the preface will remind you that if you approach a creative project with the curiosity of a child, not the expectation of an adult, things work in a much smoother and a more enjoyable fashion.

Writers are often resourceful types, so why not jot down every writing-related problem you can think of and have faced and consider how you got yourself out of it. As your writing experience increases and progresses, your solution may alter or change completely. This would be a good way to track your progress over time, and when future issues arise, you may not need to even look in your file.

Highlighted in this section are scenarios I have experienced with suggestions that may help. While not every problem you experience will be covered here, try adapting the suggestion to fit your issue.

Tip: Try creating a troubleshooting file of your own – a practical writing resource you revisit each time.

Problem: 'I'm constantly distracted.'

Try: Let's say you are utterly focused on a piece of writing, before you realise what is happening, you find you have been thinking about what to make for dinner instead. Or maybe the daily news has found its way into your mind, and you cannot stop dwelling on it. Perhaps a conversation between you and a friend is playing out repeatedly in your head. What did they really mean? What was it they said? Why did they answer that way? Maybe the distraction is a new idea while you're writing something else. If it is a new idea, empty your mind of it by jotting it down in keywords or bullet points as soon as you can. You might think you won't forget this brilliant idea, but it happens.

If the distraction is worry-based, like something you heard from the news, a conversation that has upset you, etc, try playing music in the background as you write. This extrasensory activity gives your brain a more useful distraction that will aid writing.

Problem: 'I've got so many plot lines, I'm confused.'

Try: Analysis is key. Take things back to basics and consider what was the plot originally about. Did you write a basic outline originally? If so, use that to compare how the story changed. In what way did it evolve? Is it all needed in this story? Might another story have crept in that can be written another time? Can you unpick the story to that point and park the unneeded parts?

While rewriting a novel, I had more threads than I knew what to do with, yet I felt every single one was needed. But how do you work out which are important, and which could be merged? Try writing down every character's arc in keywords, then do the same with the plot to compare the two. If you respond well to visual stimuli, print the whole manuscript and work your way through with a set of highlighters – one for each character – then, in a separate exercise, one for each story line. The principle is identical. Highlight every time that character speaks and appears in the narrative and use a different highlighter for each of the other characters. Visually, you will see how much time each character has on the page, which will help work out what is needed, what can be merged, and what is waffle. Use the same exercise with the themes. This will show where, or if, you have drifted in your storytelling and which ones can be merged. It can look like a messy exercise, but it will be worth the time you took to do it.

Being clear from the outset by using an outline, or at least story notes, will help you to keep on track with the themes used.

Problem: 'My deadline is putting me off.'

Try: During my school days, teachers issued deadlines that were, in retrospect, not healthy. Unrealistic deadlines create unbelievable and unnecessary pressure. This is not the way forward. I took that mindset with me when I was employed, associating deadlines with being punished rather than a date to work towards. Reframing the idea of deadlines helps. They are a helpful way to organise workload and productivity.

If the deadline was set by you, consider the parameters involved and be reasonable with what you can expect every day. Include time for days off, sickness, and other things outside of your control. When the date approaches, self-doubt can creep in, but remain focused to get the job done.

Holding yourself accountable or having someone do that helps, too. Accountability does not have to be the strict word it seems. It can be done in a friendly way that may just be a daily or weekly check-in by phone, or a friendly chat now and again. Just having someone else who knows what you are doing and how badly you want to complete it can be a helpful step in completing the project.

If your deadline was set by someone else and you are having a tough time sticking to it, perhaps have a chat with them to see if it can be extended.

Problem: 'I began my novel ten years ago. I'm still writing it.'

Try: Like the above problem, giving yourself a deadline and holding yourself accountable could be key here. Creative projects can linger if we let them. Are you procrastinating? Are you trying to make the manuscript perfect? Are you over-complicating editing, or dragging your feet with proofreading? Are you scared of what might come next?

After some essential self-analysis during the writing of a novel, something I often carry out while writing fiction, I realised I didn't want the story to finish because I was absolutely loving living inside the story and I did not want to say goodbye to the characters. I had spent an intense summer writing them, they felt like they were my friends. But having a story that close to being finished yet not finished is beyond frustrating. It also means that I could not move on to writing the next book. A logical person might say, 'then just write it', but it isn't always that easy. That was when I realised I needed to have someone hold me accountable. I needed an accountability buddy. I also intended to post my problem, daily progress, and word count on social media, so whomever read it would know I had not finished. For me this is highlighting myself in the worst way, forcing me to continue to completion because pride, and perhaps ego, won't allow me to be seen as lazy. Whatever the reasons behind it, it worked. The plus side of finding an ending means you can focus on other projects afterwards.

Accountability can walk hand in hand with discipline and deadlines, so enlist someone else to check in with you each day or each week but have them challenge you (in a friendly way) to get the job done. Once a novel is over, the sense of relief and that much-needed closure is incredible. It allows you to move on with a fresh mind knowing that the sense of achievement you have gained is everything. With that sense of achievement, you should remember that you also have determination, perseverance, discipline, stamina, creative skills, project management skills, and you have written a book to boot!

Problem: 'I am not disciplined.'

Try: The word 'discipline' both scares and excites us. Along with 'accountability' and 'deadline', 'discipline' might not be a word you would usually associate with a creative pursuit. However, they can all play a part in writing and finished a novel. Sometimes discipline and excitement work together, producing the energy it takes to write. Discipline brings motivation and incentive. Try reframing what discipline means to you, just like the exercise with deadlines above.

Problem: 'My manuscript is narrative heavy. Is this okay?'

Try: Possibly. It depends on the genre and the plot. Maybe the narrative is full of poetic description, which is simply your style. Some novels are narrative heavy with opulent description and yield very little dialogue, while with others it is almost like reading a script. It depends what you want out of your story, and your style of writing. There is nothing stopping you altering or completely changing your style of writing either. Try different types to see which is the next, most organic fit.

Problem: 'My characters stare at each other rather than speak. How can I make my characters talk more?'

Try: If you want your characters to speak more, have them engage in dialogue with each other rather than having them think about what they might do. Having them eyeing each other up is fine a few times providing it is right for the type of story and the plot. Have them discuss the goals they are working towards, have them ask about each other's life, what got them to this point? Create conflicts where they have no choice but to argue their way out of the situation.

The general conversations we have in everyday life are like those of the fiction world. You just need to ensure their conversations are relevant to the story and each other. Remember that it is the dialogue that tells your reader about your characters. Many readers skim over the narrative and gather the gist of the story through the dialogue. This gives you, the writer, a head start by giving lots of exciting teasers through conversations between characters.

Problem: 'How do I merge description with dialogue?'

Try: Combine them with dialogue to create engaging storytelling. Read other books to see how they do it and echo their technique in your own stories. Remember to give consideration to your page layout too by giving each character's dialogue its own line. This gives clarity to who is speaking, plus gives the reader a better visual experience.

Problem: 'How can I describe a character without making it seem obvious?'

Try: This is one of those writer issues that pops up frequently. There is somewhat of a cliché about writers using mirrors as a method by which a character looks at their reflections before a line or two of narrative describes what they look like. Sure, it has been overdone, but I don't think it ought to be completely thrown out of our toolkits. Sometimes it is appropriate. If that does not suit your needs, try having another character describe them in conversation. You can also be outright about it and simply describe them in the narrative.

Problem: 'Too many characters doing the same thing.'

Try: Firstly, you have discovered the problem already. Secondly, look at each character's reason for being in your story. What is their individual role within it? If you removed them, would it matter to the story? Are they aspects of one character? Perhaps they are all aspects of you? Try taking another look at the plot to see who is actually and truly needed to be in the story and carry out the necessary goals.

Sometimes having fewer characters is easier to deal with. As a guideline, I do not like to deal with more than half a dozen characters in my novels, but obviously that depends on the story. Some writers pull off having a huge cast while others find it tricky. If all your characters have a unique role to play, and if every one of them is developed, potentially there is no problem with having a lot. However, if you plan on publishing your novel, readers may have a tricky time keeping up with countless characters, so do make it easy to tell them apart.

There is a formula that some writers adapt to fit their stories. It could look something like this: Main character, friend, antagonist, shape shifter, guide. The first few are obvious, and as the name suggests the shape shifter is the character who will be floating around seemingly supporting the MC, or the antagonist, at any given time. They are usually the one who keeps the reader wondering which side they are on. A good example of the guide would be someone like Gandalf in *The Lord of the Rings*, who was there to help the Hobbits by guiding them onto the right path to complete their quest. Try not use the formula too much as your stories will become obvious to readers and there will be no surprises to look forward to as they will come to expect certain things. Formulaic stories have their place but be careful how you use them so your stories do not become automatically tied into the formula every time you put pen to pad.

Problem: 'Does writer's block exist?'

Try: The existence of writer's block always makes me smile because it can so easily divide a room. Throughout my time as a writer, I have met many who have at some point experienced some kind of block. Some people, not even writers themselves, will tell you that writer's block does not exist, that is it simply a name given to those lazier writers who like moaning or just prefer to sleep all day. They suggest that focusing directly on the writing is all that is needed. This would imply that instant focus is easy for everyone. But it is not.

I believe that writer's block goes way deeper than you might first imagine. Having experienced varying reasons and situations that prevented me from writing, imagining, and creating, it is probably that so much of this particular problem is down to our brains because they are so powerful that they can even work against us. We believe whatever our mind tells us is true, even when it isn't. If it provides a reasonable argument why something is or is not, we will probably believe it without even challenging it. That's how powerful they are. And that is where writer's block comes in.

Writer's block is a form of self-sabotage, and self-sabotage is exactly what is sounds like: sabotaging ourselves, preventing us from doing something we probably want to do. And, to make matters worse, it can present itself when we have a deadline to reach. Some Creatives (with a capital 'C') are sensitive people and seem to suffer from writer's block frequently. From my experience, this sensitivity allows us to align our feelings with the weather, feel empathy – and often extreme empathy for others, and experience extreme senses like the television volume being too loud, odours being too strong when other people can hardly detect them, and even sensing moods when we walk into a room. Being sensitive does not make Creative people weak, nor is it a terrible thing. In fact, it can be quite the opposite. Being in touch with our sensitivities enables some pretty amazing stories to be written because of the feelings that were conveyed. But when it affects us frequently by stopping fluid writing progress, it can be a tough pill to swallow.

Mental health issues like anxiety and depression are other ways that writer's block can present itself. From my own experiences, I know that over-stimulation can affect me. Stimulants like too much caffeine can be problematic to writing progress and show through the inability to mentally focus, which over time can bring on the block. Over-stimulation can also bring on fatigue, exhaustion, worries, etc. Some ways to counter, or even remove the block, are rest, meditation, and sleep. Self-care is a huge help.

Do always speak to a mental health professional if you need help.

Problem: 'I need to prove I can finish a book.'

Try: To whom are you trying to prove this? If it is about proving it to yourself, I can rally around that. This guide is about empowerment and creating self-confidence with creative writing. The statement highlights the fact that previous stories remain unfinished. Perhaps it would help to set boundaries so you can concentrate, find a way to motivate yourself, or have someone hold you accountable to completion. Why not try one of the creative writing exercises at the start of this book? The NaNoWriMo writing challenge in November can be a help here too because of the need to write daily to form a regular routine, and the community in which NaNoWriMo works. The momentum motivates you to continue daily, and if you have even the slightest competitive streak in you, you will want to show this on your online progress chart – which other writers can see!

If finding time to write is an issue, check out the suggestions surrounding setting writing boundaries at the start of this guide. Carving time within your schedule to write is about ensuring others do not take your allocated writing time for their needs. It is also making sure you believe your writing time is important enough to have it in your schedule in the first place.

There are other ways to finish a novel. Keep in mind that the more themes and plot lines you have in your story, the more you need to give them attention. The same goes for the amount of characters, their development, arcs, backstories, potential family trees, etc. If that feels overwhelming, perhaps keep your stories simple and your characters few. You can write a novel using one character if you wanted to.

Writing a novel takes time, discipline, and stamina to complete. Place yourself in a good position by ensuring you have intention, too. Once you have completed your novel, you can celebrate by shouting about your personal achievement from the rooftops. I am sending you a 'congratulations' in advance.

Problem: 'I'm plagued with self-doubt. I don't think readers will enjoy the story.'

Try: Remember, you cannot please everyone all the time. Self-doubt is a nasty thing. Our belief that we cannot do something can be hugely destructive. It can apply to just about everything in life, not just writing or entering into creative projects. Oddly, at times, no sooner have we given ourselves a private talking to within our heads, the thing we were convinced we could not do is done.

Tackling our inner chatter might be the first place to start. This is the voice we have inside our heads that tells us we cannot do something before we have even tried. Because creative writing projects are something of great emotional value to us or the person you are doing it for, instantly, there will be a feeling of pressure because you don't want to let anyone down, not even yourself. And that is where the self-doubt comes in. Try being open-minded. Whatever negative thought might enter your mind, counter it with something positive.

Focus on telling the story the best way you can, ensuring you complete it. Once it is published, it is out of your hands and you can put all your energies into writing the next one.

Problem: 'I don't think I'm good enough to write a book or be called a writer.'

Try: This sounds like Imposter Syndrome. In the realm of creative writing the definition would be that you don't deserve to be called a writer because, perhaps, you have not earned the right. Perhaps you have elevated the role of writer to a point that seems unrealistically high? It might also be that you feel incapable of creating that writing project because you think you lack the skills.

Some of this might come from identity. When I first published, back in 2006, I was still employed. When I highlighted to my colleagues that I had written a book, there was quite a mixed reception. Some were excited for me and wanted to read it, while others seemed quite put out that I should refer to myself as a Writer (with a capital 'W') while working on reception in their office. It made me think deeply about the title. Was I fit to call myself a writer or was I kidding myself? But then I remember I had put in years of work before I got to this point. They had just not known about it. And I had written and published a book, so that meant I was a writer. The attitudes of others often influence our own, but if you have written stories, poems, non-fiction, articles, etc, you are a writer.

Try some of the creative writing exercises in Chapter 4: Creative Writing Exercises for All Ages boost your confidence. Also try a writing group where you will meet supportive and encouraging writers of all ages and abilities. Reading other writers' work will help you see that your own writing is just as good, if not better than theirs. The result you are seeking is to feel comfortable with writing and identifying yourself as a writer.

Problem: 'I am bored with my story.'

Try: There are two ways to look at this. Are you bored with the story, or are you bored with the writing? If you are bored with your story, perhaps take things back to basics and check your original outline. Did your plot sound exciting from the start or were you hoping it would pick up some excitement along the way? While writing 'pantster' style (writing by the seat of your pants) can work, you might find it easier on yourself to keep track of things by creating an outline to start with. Check out the brainstorming exercises at the start of this guide to see where you can add some spice or excitement to your story. Think of the overall story as starting with a high, then have a breather or a low, then another high, breather, and ending on a high. This structure could help you pace your story, too.

Could your boredom be due to your characters either being flat on the page or not having much work to do? Perhaps you need to start liking your characters again? If they feel flat, try the suggestions in Chapter 5: Writing Fiction in the Creating Characters section. If you find yourself with a character who just does not have much to do, it is time to recheck the plot to see what more you can give them. Don't forget how the other characters have jobs within the story, too. One character can create obstacles for another to overcome, and there is always the idea of a love interest and all the dialogue and activity that could come along with that. While you are giving your characters something to do, ensure you are doing it for the sake of an exciting plot, not just for something to do.

If there is no saving the story or the characters, perhaps you need to park this one and start afresh with another. If so, do not discard the older story, it can be harvested for other ones. Keep a file with pieces of narrative or unfinished stories inside. You never know when they may fit another you are working on. Nothing need ever be wasted. The next time you view it, you will be in a different mindset and the story or character could work straight away.

If boredom arises during the middle part of your novel, do not panic. This is quite normal. Sometimes there is a lull, and your attention falls away. While it is possible you may need to take a break, especially for your energy and imagination levels to rest, story middles take a fair chunk of work. This happens to all writers. We can only put out so much content before we need to regroup. If a break is neither necessary nor practical, there are ways to proceed and keep your interest. The middle is the link between the start and the end, so go back to basics and highlight the themes with which you started the story. If you already know the ending, join them up with the start.

Perhaps taking a week or two off from your novel will help, even taking a six-month break might work. Resetting your brain and allowing your imagination to refuel may be just what you need. In the meantime, if your craft urge won't leave you, why not turn your hand to a different creative activity, something more practical? In my downtime from writing, I turn my hand to crafts, needlework, dressmaking, acrylic painting, and other things. Maybe they can help you, too?

Problem: 'How do I make people buy my book?'

Try: That is the big question! Although you cannot make anyone buy your book, you can entice them to want to. I would argue though that there are easier ways to make money than writing, so if that is your goal, you may need to rethink. If it is about getting some interest, you will need to think about marketing your book when you start writing it. Knowing who your audience is will be a massive help to knowing who might buy it once it is complete. Having an author website and linking posts to social media can help your marketing campaign, and later on nearer the time you want to publish (in whichever form you choose), you can take more steps with bigger and more invasive marketing.

Other ways exist to promote your book to the right audience. Don't forget to get physical with your marketing campaign by not relying entirely on social media. Giving talks to community groups helps get your name and book known locally and holding book signings, too, perhaps in book shops, libraries, pubs, and cafes. Community radio stations are usually interested in interviewing local authors, as are regional radio stations. Podcasters and YouTube hosts may also show interest if your book aligns with their audience.

There are a plethora of books and marketing advice out in the world, so conduct a researching session to see what appeals to you and the themes within your book.

Problem: 'I want to write a book, I just don't want to publish it.'

Try: I love this. Just because you have written, does not mean you need to publish. Writing for yourself is entirely your choice, and some books are not meant for the eyes of others. Never feel pressurised into publishing if it is not for you.

Problem: 'I keep altering the genre I want to write in. I just cannot stick to one.'

Try: I totally get this. Not every writer has just one specific genre in which they write. You may think of a story to develop that falls into the crime genre, then later find you get an idea for a horror story or a romance. A walk in a forest might conjure a children's adventure with animals that speak and trees that walk, but the last story you wrote was a romance. Ideas, in whichever way they arrive in our imaginations, do not always fit into one category.

Each story might drift into a different genre, too, known as genre blending. Or you might write a funny crime novel that would fall into crime and have a sub-genre of comedy. Unless you are under contract to write something specific, you can alter your stories to your tastes any time you please. It is why we call it creative writing. Don't fight it, be open-minded and see what happens and where it takes you.

Problem: 'Focusing my mind is tough.'

Try: For many writers it very much is tough. With countless distractions, both from other people and from technology, it seems we find more and more reasons to be on alert. Trying to settle into your writing or focus on a specific part can be tricky. However, check out the timed exercises in Chapter 4: Creative Writing Exercises for All Ages for some challenges that can excite us enough to focus. Add the timer for extra focus.

If writing exercises are not your thing or you just want to focus on your MS, set yourself a few minutes at a time to write and work your way up to bigger sessions. By doing this you can ease your mind into focusing on one thing, and perhaps trick it into working. Set the timer to five, ten or fifteen minutes at first. See how that progresses and if it works well move on to thirty minutes, then forty-five, then sixty. Do not stop until the alarm has gone off.

Problem: 'I'm worried my ideas will vanish.'

Try: Understandably, our ideas are the very things that create books. Don't fret though, because when we get an idea, the act of simply jotting it down through keywords or bullet points will enable us to pick it right up again when we are free to do so.

Problem: 'I'm procrastinating too much.'

Try: Of course, you want to write, but something is stopping you. Chances are you know what it is, too. So why do we do this to ourselves? Finding things to do in place of writing that story or that book is something that affects almost all writers. It could be that you don't quite know where to begin, or that the end or middle of the project is shouting at you more than the start. Or that you want it to be completely perfect from the outset. Maybe you are about to start writing but before you get to it you just need to get the house in order. Perhaps get the housework done. And the dusting. And the vacuuming, even add a splash of paint to the walls. Perhaps your spare room would make a great writing room, so clearing it out will help to create some space for a desk or table for you to work at.

It is so easy to get involved in other things, so try using a timer to allow yourself an hour to do those other things if they absolutely need doing then focus on your writing. Wouldn't it be wonderful at the end of a writing session to focus on the story you created, rather than looking at clean skirting boards?

Problem: 'How do I know which tense and point of view to write it?'

Try: Tense is the way that shows how time is moving. Past, present, and future tenses are the three basic ways, but there are more worth researching. Past and present are the most popular in fiction, but each have their limitations. Past tense can give the reader a detached feeling like they are reading about something someone else has experienced, whereas present tense gives a more immediate feeling.

Point of view is through whose eyes we read the story. Marrying the two together can create a distance or more immersive reading experiences. Perhaps experiment with both to see how best your story is conveyed. Re-read it once finished in case the tenses have been merged without you realising as this can be easily done.

Problem: 'My pace is patchy. How can I keep it consistent?'

Try: Keeping an eye on your pacing can help a story create tension in the thrilling parts and give the reader a breather in the parts in between. If you focus on the major events happening within your story, you will be able to see where the tension is tight or loose. If you don't feel any thrills or see any tension created, perhaps look at where it falls.

Try keeping things interesting and exciting in the storytelling, and when it comes to editing ensure you remove filler words. Fillers are those that are not needed like 'really' in really funny, 'very' in very hard, and other words that emphasise the adjective. Choose weightier words instead like 'hilarious' or 'tough'.

Ensure your pace is appropriate for the genre. A young adult or crime story may work well with shorter, punchier sentences, while a romantic story that might require highs and lows in its pacing can benefit from short and longer sentences. Using this technique also adds to the visuals and gives variety to the reader.

Problem: 'Is punctuation really necessary?'

Try: Punctuation is vital within your novel. Punctuation tells the reader where you want them to pause and stop, identify who is speaking, and where tension lies, what is a surprise or shock piece of narrative or dialogue, and where questions are. Think of punctuation as a code or message from you to them telling them how best to consume your work. Other pieces of punction like the semi-colon, ellipsis, bracket, etc might not be used often but they still have a place. Brackets are mostly used in non-fiction, and both the semi-colon ';' and the ellipsis '…' have definitive jobs to carry out, so I believe they still have a place in our literary toolboxes.

For clarification, the semi-colon is to be used like a comma or full stop, depending on what you want from the joining sentences. The ellipsis, or ellipses to use its plural, is a magical tool that behaves in multiple ways. One shows that time is passing or has passed, as shown in the example below, which helps create a sense of tension. You can use it during dialogue too, to show speech trailing off: 'I wanted to tell you, but I just …'

Problem: 'How can I create tension in my thriller?'

Try: Tension can be created through word choice, pacing, and a good plot. Never overlook the use of punctuation as a great tension creating tool either. Here's an example during narrative, 'Davenport hovered cautiously. The red numbers counted down. Ten … Nine … Eight …' You can also use ellipses in the narrative to show different events are happening simultaneously. 'Nixon prayed Davenport had already diffused the bomb. Would there still be time to get the crew into their shuttles? Seven … Six … Five … . Taking a massive gamble, she snipped the green wire. Four … Three … Then nothing. "Did we do it?" she yelled.' Using ellipses this way adds to the tension created by the already tense moment of disarming a bomb on a spaceship.

Problem: 'My horror story isn't scary enough.'

Try: What one considers scary is not what others will consider scary because opinions on fear and other feelings are subjective. Depending on your themes, maybe it's a boo-scare or gore you are after. Perhaps it's more psychological than that? Try thinking about how film-makers convey fear in their movies. Often, it is through characters' behaviour and how they treat others rather than the setting, although how you describe a location can be frightening. Horror is conveyed through the characters' response to imagery, so go wild with creating pictures inside your readers' minds.

Creating tension can be down to the word choice, so consider using a thesaurus to find alternative words with sinister meanings.

Psychological horror provides tension and thrills in both literature and scriptwriting. Give some thought to your character development to see how they behave and what their motives are for doing so. Try some of the character development and brainstorming writing exercises in Chapter 4: Creative Writing Exercises for All Ages to see how creepy and/or scary you can make a character's personality. If you frighten yourself, you are off to a good start.

Problem: 'What is passive and active writing?'

Try: Passive writing detaches us slightly from what is happening in a story, whereas active writing drops us right into the action. For example:

- Passive: the hat was worn on his head.
- Active: he wore the hat.
- Passive: chess was played by the boys.
- Active: the boys played chess.
- Passive: the estate was damaged by the storm.
- Active: the storm damaged the estate.

Problem: 'I've written myself into a corner.'

Try: This is quite common. We get so involved with the story that we can forget to keep to the path. If you have written yourself into a corner and cannot find a way to get your characters back on their way, take a step back and look at your work with editor's eyes. Can you identify where it began to get stuck? Can you unpick the manuscript back to that point before rewriting out of the corner? Once you have identified the moment, rewrite away from it back on track. If the tangent highlights some interesting narrative or dialogue, do not delete it. Keep it in a special file for these things so you can salvage some of your efforts.

Problem: 'How long should I make my chapters?'

Try: Chapters ought not to be a prescriptive length. Unless a publisher has contracted you to write specific lengths for your chapters, they do not have a standard length. Chapters are there to separate the scenes into readable chunks. They also give a breath to the reader (and writer). While some chapters fall naturally with the same word count, it is more unlikely than likely that this will happen. To create a prescriptive length for every chapter would make the story overly formulaic. By making each chapter five thousand or ten thousand words long, you will be filling it unnecessarily and if the scene takes longer than the prescriptive length, you won't have space to finish the scene.

Allow your chapters to be the length they need to be to tell that section of the story. It helps to illustrate this if you are a visual person. Think of your story as a movie or TV show, when each scene is over that is when your chapter should end.

Write the scene and finish the chapter, however long or short it is. Some big names have used just half a page for a chapter to progress their story and others have written fifty pages. The same principle is true with your sentences and paragraphs. A mixture of lengths adds variety.

Problem: 'I keep being interrupted.'

Try: Unexpected guests, whether family or friends, can be irritating when you are trying to focus on writing, and because you love them dearly you will probably add guilt to the mix. Try to create a specific time and space to write. If people just won't leave you be, you may have to be blunt and ask them to respect your writing time. Remember you can spend time in a coffee shop, or your local library as mentioned previously.

Problem: 'I keep comparing myself with other writers. It's bringing me down.'

Try: While healthy comparisons can be helpful, unhealthy ones are destructive. Firstly, an unhealthy comparison may take the shape of thinking you will never be as good at writing as this author. But let's put that into perspective. If the author is a big name, let's say in fiction, then they will have years of experience under their belt, and will also have had a team of people assisting them. Within this team there will be editors, typesetters, cover artists, etc, so while it looks like they created the whole book themselves, they had help. The chances are you don't. So, comparing your work with theirs is, you can now see, unfair to you.

Secondly, there is such a thing as a healthy comparison. This could be where you read a chapter of a book, whether it is fiction or non-fiction, and analyse where the tone or mood is created. Maybe you can spot how they created tension in a specific paragraph, how they created a character with depth and drive. Possibly the pacing is the aspect you are drawn to? Identifying these techniques is a good skill to learn so you may adapt it to your own style of creative writing. So, rather that viewing the comparison as a negative, see the differences as a positive instead.

There is no other writer quite like you. Be confident in your skills and develop self-belief in your stories.

Problem: 'How many words are in which genre?'

- Flash fiction – up to 500 words
- Short story – up to 10,000 words
- Novella – approximately 40,000 words
- Novel lengths vary due to differing genres, stories, and author styles, but approximate figures are:
- Crime/thriller: 90–100k
- Romance: 80–100k
- Fantasy: 100k+
- Science fiction: 80k–100k
- Young adult: 40k
- Children's fiction: up to 1,000 words depending on age and story style. A picture book may be approximately 50 words, but stories intended to be read with a parent or guardian might be nearer the 1,000-word mark.

Problem: 'Should I rewrite my story?'

Try: Possibly. Rewriting is another form of editing. Sometimes stories need to be written from a different character's point of view. Perhaps the story feels restricted and the characters cannot move or see or hear because it was originally in the wrong tense or point of view. Sometimes you need to write a story to discover whose it really is. From whose lips is it being told? The only way to know for sure is if you rewrite it. It can take time, but consider it an investment in the creation of the book and if you adore the story it will be worth the time spent.

Problem: 'Should I have a launch party if it is my first book?'

Try: Absolutely, why not? You have worked on the MS and given it time and effort so you ought to celebrate its completion. That said, launch parties are not for everyone. I have experienced several different kinds over the years; my own and those of other authors. Some have been small, intimate affairs, while others were attended by hundreds of people. Sometimes there are glasses of bubbly and other times it's more of a plastic beaker event. Whatever suits your needs, your budget, and your style, enjoy it. Congratulations!

Take Away Tips from this Chapter

- Every writer has literary challenges somewhere along the line.
- Create your own troubleshooting resource.
- Make healthy comparisons. Avoid unhealthy ones.
- Enjoy your creative process.

Chapter 10

Publishing Options

In a book that hails creative writing as a way of life, whether that takes the role of hobby or career, it makes sense to include a little information on publishing options. There have been significant leaps in publishing over the past decade. Traditional publishing is no longer the only way forwards. Independent publishing allows authors to take control of their own work and publish their book their way, keeping the majority of the profits.

That said, it is still worth remembering that while publishing might be right for you and your book, please don't ever feel you have to publish your work. Some projects are not made for the eyes of the public, or even for friends and family. Some projects are just for you and are complete simply by being created.

What does publishing mean?

Publishing is the act by which your work is put out into the public domain for reading and selling. Fortunately, over the past decade or two, publishing options have evolved, giving writers a wider choice and ability to control their literary careers.

Traditional Publishing

As the name suggestions, traditional publishing is the usual way books are published. The kinds you see in supermarkets, book shops, and libraries have been traditionally published. This means the author submitted their MS to an agent, or directly to a publisher where appropriate, and the agent sells it to a publishing house. It is worth a mention here that this is a very simplified definition; the actual process requires a lot more research, work, and time.

Usually, the author will research literary agents who represent the genre in which he or she has written their story. If the agent believes they can sell the novel, the author is signed, and a publishing house sought. From contract signing to publishing takes approximately a year, sometimes more. Traditional publishing houses make decisions about the book, its rights, its contents, title, and deal with cover design. While they may assist with marketing the book, the author is usually expected to do much of it themselves. The author may receive an advance and a percentage of the sale of each book known as royalties. How big the advance is usually falls to how big the publisher is and the expected number of book sales. While it might be the dream of a first-time writer to get rich from their novel, it is extremely rare for a debut author to hit the jackpot with a large publisher and receive a huge advance.

Independent Publishing

This means the author submits their book to a small press who has signed multiple authors. Both the publisher and author discuss the contents, titles, and cover design. Some presses will assist with marketing, but it is usually up to the author to get this done. An agreed percentage of each sale goes to the author through royalties.

Self-publishing

This is when the authors publish their own books through print-on-demand services, directly to Amazon or other large book-selling bodies. It is the author's decision on how the contents look, their choice on the title, and the cover design. It is fair to say that, since the advent of self-publishing ten or fifteen years ago, there are a lot of books available that, perhaps, ought not to be. Based on their quality in the areas of editing, proofreading, cover choice, story and character development, etc, some books have been published before they are ready. For many authors, only experience will highlight the errors, but with experience, research, and adopting a professional stance by viewing the book as a business product, most authors hit the mark perfectly.

Publishing this way means, providing the books sells, the author keeps the majority of the profit with a percentage of the sale going to the platform they have used to publish or market the book. The author takes full responsibility for marketing their book. To help with being noticed for the right reasons, please give serious consideration to hiring an independent editor and cover designer unless, of course, you have considerable experience in both these areas yourself.

You can find out more information about self-publishing via the Alliance of Independent Authors.

Hybrid Publishing

This is a merging of both independent and self-publishing. The publisher and the author usually put up half the money to publish and market the book, but share the profits, too.

Vanity Publishing

An author pays (usually) thousands of pounds to get their book published and receive several hundred copies to sell themselves. Vanity publishers are not generally well considered as some prey on vulnerable writers offering them what seems like a very lucrative deal. It is not. Please always do your research before you take the next step in publishing your book.

How do I Find an Agent or Publisher?

The suggested ways to find an agent or publisher for your manuscript is to check *The Writers' and Artists' Yearbook*. There are physical copies available in most UK libraries and it is on sale in all good bookshops. Even though the yearbook's information is good for the year it is published, previous years' copies may still be correct. If you have your heart set on a specific publisher and the yearbook provides guidelines that tick all your boxes, check the publisher's website to ensure nothing has changed.

Social media can be a big help, too, especially X, formerly Twitter, because there are often hashtag pitch sessions that invite writers to send a pitch of their manuscripts. Publishers trawl through reading the pitches that, at X's word limit, means they are quick to move through. From the writer's point of view, it gives you a great opportunity to be seen and make your pitch as interesting yet brief as possible. If an agent is interested, they will contact you through X.

There are several festivals that take place every year in which publishers and agents participate. Check online for those that are appropriate for your genre and location.

What are Submission Guidelines?

If you decide to enter your work into a competition or submit your book to a literary agent or publishing house, you will need to seek out and follow their submission guidelines. These are the competition judges', literary agents', or publishing houses' rules of submission. They tell you exactly how they want to consume your work. Guidelines often include word count, font style, closing dates, accepted genres, etc. If a guideline suggests they want a thriller of forty thousand words in Times New Roman with the deadline of 31 December 2024, please do not send them a romance of eighty thousand words in Comic Sans by 10 August 2025.

You will usually be invited to send a synopsis, cover letter, and the first three chapters via email. However, while the majority of publishers expect the MS to be sent electronically, there is still a tiny portion who prefer hard copies send through the post. Do check what the publisher requires. They are very busy people so if yours is the MS that does not fit their requirements, it may not even be seen. Give yourself every possible chance to be seen.

Ensure you have edited and proofread your submission. Follow submission guidelines to the letter, making sure there is nothing about your submission that will hold it back. It will be competing for attention with many others, so ensuring yours is polished and the best it can be puts you in a good position straight away.

Before you submit, go through the brief again, and the submission guidelines, too. Sometimes we get so caught up in the story or poem that we may go off on a tangent, but if that was not part of the original brief you may lose your chance to be noticed.

How long you should wait for a response is not an exact science. Publishers are extremely busy people and don't usually have much time to respond to hopeful authors unless they want to represent them. Some publishers respond within the day, others may take over a year. Depending on the size of the publishing house and a host of other variables, it can take months. Some publishing houses actually tell you this in their submission guidelines but many don't. My advice would be to submit your MS, and forget all about it. If it comes back a 'yes', fantastic. If there is no response at all after four or five months, try prodding them gently with a polite email. If they don't respond to this, it may be a sign that your book is not well placed for that publishing house. If they do respond, at least you will have a better appreciation of where you stand.

Copyright

Copyright is an interesting area that has been created for the protection of your work. For information on how it affects you, check out www.gov.uk/government/organisations/intellectual-property-office

Take Away Tips from this Chapter

- Never be afraid to ask – nobody is born knowing everything.
- Research which method of publishing is best for you and your book.
- One size does not fit all.
- Give serious thought to hiring help before you publish your book.

Resources

Some useful resources referred to within this book.

Alliance of Independent Authors, c/o The Free Word Centre, 60 Farringdon Road, London, EC1R 3GA, http://allianceindependentauthors.org

British Library, 96 Euston Road, London, NW1 2DB, www.bl.uk

British Library Legal Deposit Library, Boston Spa, Wetherby, LS23 7BY, www.bl.uk/aboutus/stratpolprog/legaldep

Chartered Institute of Editing and Proofreading, Studio 206, Milton Keynes Business Centre, Foxhunter Drive, Linford Wood, Milton Keynes, Buckinghamshire, MK14 6GD, www.ciep.uk

Nielsen UK ISBN, 3rd Floor, Midas House, 62, Goldworth Road, Woking, Surrey, GU21 6LQ

www.isbn.nielsenbookdata.co.uk. Official ISBN agency for the UK

Society of Authors, 84 Drayton Gardens, London, SW10 9SB, www.societyofauthors.org

UK Copyright Service, 4 Tavistock Avenue, Didcot, Oxfordshire, OX11 8NA, www.copyrightservice.co.uk

Intellectual Property Office,
www.gov.uk/government/organisations/intellectual-property-office

Essex Libraries, www.essex.gov.uk

Bibliography

Banham, S.J., 2023, *I've Got a Pen and I'm Not Afraid to Use it*, Second Edition, Milton Keynes. For the Love of Books.

Ackerman, A, and Puglisi, B., 2013, *The Positive Trait Thesaurus: A Writer's Guide to Character Attributes*, JADD Publishing.

Banham, S.J., 2007, *Dicing With Danger*, Essex: Basildon Printing Company.

Banham, S.J., 2022, *Dream State*, Essex: For the Love of Books.

Banham, S.J., 2008, *Guardian Angel*, Essex: Basildon Printing Company.

Banham, S.J., 2018, Ghosting!, Essex: For the Love of Books.

Banham, S.J., 2007, *Jenna's Dad*, Essex: Basildon Printing Company.

Banham, S.J., 2021, *Livin' and Lovin' in Texas*, Essex: For the Love of Books.

Banham, S.J., 2018, *Writing Naked: Writing Without Boundaries. Volume One*, Essex: For the Love of Books.

Blanchard, G., 2020, *Writing Your Family History: A Guide For Family Historians*, Barnsley: Pen and Sword.

Crofts, A., 2004, *Ghostwriting*, London: A & C Black Publishers Limited.

King, S., 2000, *On Writing: A Memoir of the Craft*, London: Hodder and Stoughton.

Obstfeld, R., and, Neumann, F., 2002, *Careers for your Characters: A Writer's Guide to 101 Professions from Architect to Zookeeper*, Ohio: F&W Publications Inc.

Spellman, A., 2021, *Bookbinding and How to Bring Old Books Back to Life*, Barnsley: Pen and Sword Limited.

Montgomery, L.M. (Lucy Maud), 1989. *Anne of Green Gables*, Boston: Godine.

Fielding, H., 1999, *Bridget Jones's Diary: a novel*, New York: Penguin Books.

Townsend, S., 2002, *The Secret Diary of Adrian Mole Aged 13¾*, New York: Penguin Books.

Rowling, J.K., 2014, *Harry Potter and The Half-Blood Prince*, London: Bloomsbury Children's Books.

Pepys, Samuel, 1932, *Samuel Pepys' Diary*, New York: De Luxe Editions.

Frank, A., 1989, *The Diary of Anne Frank*, Chicago: New Longman Literature.

Tolkien, J.R.R., 1991, *The Lord of The Rings*, England: HarperCollins.

Websites

For the Love of Books, www.loveofbooks.co.uk

Society of Authors, www2.societyofauthors.org

Alliance of Independent Authors, www.allianceindependentauthors.org

Amazon, www.amazon.com, booksellers and e-book publishers

Pen and Sword Books, www.pen-and-sword.co.uk

Facebook, www.facebook.com

LinkedIn, www.linkedin.com

X (formerly Twitter), https://twitter.com

Ancestry, https://ancestry.co.uk

Magazines

Writing Magazine, www.writers-online.co.uk

Writers and Artists, www.writersandartists.co.uk

Recommended Reading

Bookbinding and How to Bring Old Books Back to Life, Aimee Spellman

Can You Make the Title Bigga, Jessica Bell

Careers for your Characters: A Writer's Guide to 101 Professions from Architect to Zookeeper, Raymond Obstfeld and Franz Neumann

On Writing, Stephen King

Ghost Writing, Andrew Crofts

Ghosting!, S.J. Banham

I've Got a Pen and I'm Not Afraid to Use It, S.J. Banham

The Positive Trait Thesaurus: A Writer's Guide to Character Attributes, Angela Ackerman and Becca Puglisi

Writing Your Family History: A Guide for Family Historians, Gill Blanchard

Recommended Listening

Alliance of Independent Authors podcast
Society of Authors podcast
The Versatile Writer podcast
Write Now podcast

Index